A GOD
DIVIDED

A GOD DIVIDED

UNDERSTANDING THE DIFFERENCES BETWEEN ISLAM, CHRISTIANITY, AND JUDAISM

CHRISTOPHER CATHERWOOD

The Bible Teacher's Teacher

COOK COMMUNICATIONS MINISTRIES
Colorado Springs, Colorado • Paris, Ontario
KINGSWAY COMMUNICATIONS LTD
Eastbourne, England

Victor® is an imprint of
Cook Communications Ministries, Colorado Springs, CO 80918
Cook Communications, Paris, Ontario
Kingsway Communications, Eastbourne, England

A GOD DIVIDED
© 2007 by Christopher Catherwood

Published in association with the literary agency of Jan P. Dennis, 19350 Glen
Hollow Circle, Monument, CO 80132.

Cover Design: Amy Kiechlin
Interior Design: Karen Athen

First Printing, 2007
Printed in the United States of America

1 2 3 4 5 6 7 8 9 10

ISBN 978-0-7814-4374-6
LCCN 2006933449

✡ ✟ ☪

Contents

✡   ✝   ☾

The spelling of many ancient Middle Eastern names is notoriously inconsistent. The same applies to many Islamic names and places. This is because they're written in a completely different alphabet, and different languages have translated them in very diverse ways. Is it Qur'an; Quran; Koran; or, to use a French spelling, Coran? Is it Muhammad; Mahommed; or, to use the Turkish Muslim way of spelling his name, Mehmet?

Unfortunately, there's no standard spelling. Eagle-eyed readers will notice that even the terrorist group al-Qaeda (or Al Qaida) is sometimes spelled differently, depending on the newspaper or journal one is reading. Their leader is Osama bin Laden or, in some cases, Usama bin Ladin.

The same applies to the spelling of some Old Testament figures and their contemporaries, such as Egyptian pharaohs.

I've aimed to be consistent within this book on how people and places are spelled, but this is to say that if you have seen it spelled differently, both variants are probably equally correct.

Preface

✡ ✝ ☪

I'll start where most authors end, by thanking my wife, Paulette Catherwood. She is my constant support, my soul mate, my companion, my inspiration, and far more besides. She embodies that amazing woman we read about in Proverbs 31—living proof that such people can and do exist.

I'll also thank my church home group, or small-group Bible study (as it would be called in the United States). They have been faithful in prayer for every book I've written since Paulette and I joined our church, St. Andrew the Great, in 1991. Thank you to other former group members I didn't have space to mention in the dedication.

Also fully deserving thanks is our church's staff. In particular, Mark Ashton, the vicar, has been a model of biblical, expository preaching, for which thousands of us over the years have been more than grateful. Robin and Marion Porter Goff and June Morgan, older members of the congregation (most of whom are Cambridge University students), have been models of kindness and support.

Thinking of older people, my parents, Fred and Elizabeth Catherwood, who between them have had more than 120 years of Christian ministry, have been supportive in many ways, including their providing a loft office in their fifteenth-century house after I lost my office in Cambridge. They have modeled Christian marriage and service to countless people throughout the world, notably through their ministry in the International Fellowship of Evangelical Students (my father is a former treasurer and my mother a current vice president).

Paulette's father, Rev. John Moore, served in ministry for more than sixty years, finally retiring from the editorship of a Baptist journal at age eighty-three! He was the perfect father-in-law and, like my parents, an inspiration to countless Christian men and women over the decades.

This book was inspired through my contact with literary agent Jan Dennis. Jan is a well-known figure in Christian publishing and also a prominent jazz critic. I've had the pleasure of knowing many of the Dennis family over the past twenty years, ever since Jan and his brother Lane were kind enough to publish one of my early books. My thanks to Jan and the entire Dennis clan are profound.

Editors deserve all the thanks they can get. (I used to be one before I went back to academic life.) This book was delayed due to my overcommitment on some other projects, so I'm especially grateful to my superb editor at David C. Cook, Craig Bubeck, for his kindness, forbearance, insights, and skill.

A GOD DIVIDED

I'm fortunate to be linked to two first-class universities. The first is the University of Cambridge, where there has been a strong Christian witness now for many centuries (the great Puritan Richard Sibbes, had a close connection with my church). As a student I went to Bible studies on the staircase where the illustrious Puritan leader Oliver Cromwell had similarly studied the Bible as a student some 350 years earlier. I'm also grateful to the master and fellows of St. Edmund's College, Cambridge, for providing a great base and for many a stimulating chat over coffee in the Senior Combination Room and also to the former master, Sir Brian Heap. The Institute of Continuing Education at Madingley Hall is a great institution for which to teach, and Linda Fisher deserves thanks for giving me so many great pupils over the years.

In the United States, I'm an annual writer-in-residence for the history department of the University of Richmond, in Richmond, Virginia, and an annual teacher at their School of Continuing Studies' summer school. The quality of both the support I receive and the students I teach is outstanding. So many people at Richmond personify kindness that it would be invidious to single out individuals, but they know who they are, and my annual gratitude to them is very deep!

Last but by no means least, I teach for an American institution in Cambridge, the Institute of Economic and Political Studies (INSTEP). Professor Geoffrey Williams and his wife, Janice, are much loved on both sides of the Atlantic, and students from places such as Tulane, Wake Forest, Villanova, and many other universities have been great fun to teach. Also connected to INSTEP is another internationally known academic, Professor Maggie Bailey of Point Loma Nazarene University in California. She is both a friend to the Armenian people and a great prayer warrior, and her prayers for my work over many years are very much appreciated.

—Christopher Catherwood

A GOD DIVIDED

✡ ✝ ☪

Until the cataclysmic events of September 11, 2001, many in the West were only loosely aware of other religions and what their adherents believed. This was perhaps less true of Europe, where millions of Muslims, Hindus, and followers of a panoply of faiths have settled in recent years. But most Americans knew of other religions (apart from Judaism) in theory but knew very little of them in practice, simply because their adherents either kept to themselves or were few in number. While big cities such as New York or San Francisco had Chinatowns, for example, the great monotheistic faith of Islam made very little impression, if any, on the average American town or its citizens.

September 11 changed that permanently, but not necessarily in a good way. The event was so violent and the damage to America's psyche, a country whose homeland for the most part has been immune to the horrors of war, was so great that a distorted picture of Islam has emerged as a result. Either people now see a warm, fuzzy picture in which differences between Christianity and Islam are seriously underplayed, or they see every Muslim as a foaming-at-the-mouth killer, out to destroy the West and all who live in it. Both these stereotypes are dangerously wrong, and one thing this book should accomplish is to put forward a more balanced picture, so we can actually understand what's going on and why.

I had the interesting privilege of living in the United States as a visitor from Britain in September 2001. I spent that fall at the University of Virginia in Charlottesville on a secular Rockefeller Fellowship but still had the chance to interact daily with many of the wonderful Christians who teach there. One of these, Larry Adams, is in fact an expert in Islam; and having his political, strategic, and acute spiritual insights all at the same time was more than valuable. Except for Larry, I was struck by how little Christians knew about their own faith in relation to the two other major monotheistic faiths—Judaism and Islam.

By the ironic nature of its title—*A God Divided*—this book presumes two things:

First, there is *one* true God who is indivisible.

Second, the true faith in that God is Christianity.

In this book, to use a well-known American media phrase, I aim to be as "fair and balanced" as possible. But at the same time, I'm not pretending to be neutral—I'm a practicing Christian, and I believe that Christianity alone has the full answer. Readers should therefore proceed with that understanding.

Why am I addressing these three faiths? After 9/11,

Judaism, Christianity, and Islam became known as the three "Abrahamic" faiths (after the great Jewish patriarch who is revered equally by all three religions). Secular books aimed to accentuate the positive in a spirit of peace and ecumenism and tried to find the common ground between the three religions. Mutual reverence for Abraham is one key area of overlap.

From the point of view of trying to engender peace in a war-torn world, this attempt is fully understandable, as was President George W. Bush's declaration in a Washington DC mosque not long after 9/11 that Islam is a religion of peace. For many Muslims today, especially those living well-integrated lives in the United States, this is indeed true.

But from a spiritual viewpoint, the situation is not so simple. Obviously, people should live in peace and harmony with one another. As Jesus said, "Blessed are the peacemakers" (Matt. 5:9). But what has worried me ever since September 2001 is that two very different issues are being confused here: peace and truth.

I have the honor and privilege of knowing brave Muslims who are doing everything possible to reach out to the Christian and Jewish communities in both Britain and the United States in the name of a peaceful version of Islam. From a political and community viewpoint, this is wonderful news, since anything that can be done to increase peace between neighbors is surely good. But the problem is that many secular people then go on to say that there's no real difference between the three major faiths that believe in one God only. That, however, is not true. My peace activist Muslim friends don't even believe that themselves. In fact, they would say that Islam is a religion of both peace and truth. If they are correct, by definition Judaism and Christianity cannot be the truth, since each also claims to possess universal and absolute truth.

A God Divided was therefore written with this very question in mind—which faith is true, and why?

In our pluralistic, postmodern age, suggesting that there is but one true faith is not a popular thing to do! So I should say here that I greatly respect my many friends who profess other faiths or no faith at all. I'm enthusiastically in favor of interreligious peace and reconciliation and laud all efforts to produce it. But I do believe one can simultaneously support these peace efforts and affirm that only one faith—Christianity—is absolutely true. In fact, many Muslims and Jews feel the same about the Christian faith. It's usually those of no faith at all who are upset by claims of absolute truth, which are made most loudly by the two actively evangelistic monotheistic religions, Christianity and Islam.

I should say that I've been trained as a historian and that history informs my approach. The Bible is very much a book of history, and all three faiths should be seen in the context of how they began in particular times and places. We can also see how the respective religions have changed and the difference the seventeenth-century Protestant Reformation made to Christianity.

We will therefore look at

- the respective histories of the three faiths;
- the ways these three faiths developed over time; and, in particular,
- the ways they changed as a result of their respective reformations.

Finally, we will look at how some key issues of our time, such as science, have affected each faith's claims to absolute truth.

I hope therefore that this book enables Christians to understand the merits of their own faith better and to grasp what the other two monotheistic religions, Judaism and Islam, believe in relation to Christianity. We as Christians have no need to fear other religions: We are all humans searching to fill the same spiritual need. If this book helps even a few people better understand the truth of the Christian gospel message in relationship to these other religions, then I will have accomplished my goal.

FAITH IN ONE GOD

✡   ✝   ☪

The history of the Jews, the Old Testament people of God, begins with the call to a faithful man named Abram (who would later become Abraham), the ancestor of the Jewish race, to leave the city of Ur.

Here, however, we're not looking as much at the history of the people as of the faith. So let us look at how Judaism, the faith of the Jewish people, developed.

THE ABRAHAMIC FAITHS

Judaism, Christianity, and Islam are, in these politically correct times, often known as the three "Abrahamic" faiths. This is understandable in the sense that they all look back to and revere Abraham. A *New York Times* best seller by American radio commentator Bruce Feiler is called *Abraham: A Journey to the Heart of Three Faiths.*[†]

The Abraham described here, as Feiler admits openly, is not the person portrayed in the Bible. To such modern commentators, he is instead a kind of everyman figure, someone who found God but also challenged him—a warm, fuzzy person all people of goodwill can unite around in these troubled, terrorist times.

No one is more in favor of peace and reconciliation than I am. I know of brave Jews and Christians active for peace in Palestine, where they often risk their lives at the hands of extremists who wish death and conflict to continue. Brave Muslims in Britain and elsewhere are similarly speaking for peaceful coexistence, for being good neighbors to Westerners rather than killing them. All this bravery is wonderful news; and, in an age of terrorism and uncertainty, we can all both applaud and pray for their efforts.

But this kind of postmodern, twenty-first-century Abrahamic figure is someone made in the image of modern people who reject the very notion of a faith that can be absolutely and universally true. This kind of re-creation of the past plays well in the media—Feiler was on television a great deal back in 2002—and in many academic circles too.

But how does this cool version of Abraham—a man living on the edge, according to Feiler—go down with the

---

[†] My 2004 paperback edition (Harper Perennial) has a study guide and a chapter on how all can claim Abraham for themselves, especially after 9/11.

A GOD DIVIDED

countless millions of people worldwide today for whom Abraham is a real, scriptural figure? What of the faithful believers who trust he genuinely existed, unlike those such as Feiler, who doubt his flesh-and-blood authenticity? What of those people for whom he is a person and a powerful inspiration, not a concept?

Jews, Christians, and then Muslims, all down through the centuries, have believed that Abraham truly existed as Scripture says he did.

But, of course, it's not that simple. For, as we will discover, each of the three faiths sees a very different Abraham. Muslims, furthermore, have changed his story considerably in important theological details—and then claimed that Jews and Christians made the distortions.

In this book, we will link Abraham—a real figure, just as the Bible describes him—to other key Old Testament characters, just as faithful Jews and Christians have done over the millennia. Then we will connect him to the person central to the whole of Scripture, Jesus Christ. For while we all fully share the desire of good, well-meaning people like Feiler to bring peace and reconciliation, it cannot be done by denying the deeply held religious beliefs of millions of people.

WHAT ABRAHAM SYMBOLIZED

Since the traumatic events of 9/11 in America and 7/7 in the United Kingdom, many people in both countries have become interested in religion, especially those religions that originated in the Middle East. This is good news, as we all need to be far more aware of the world in which we live, all the more since the immunity from serious violence enjoyed by much of the West is now effectively over.

But millions of believers, including those committing atrocities, hold to a version of their faith that they believe is absolutely true. Therefore, having a diluted, mushy concept of "Well, surely we all believe the same thing, really" won't bring about the peace we all desire.

Nor, ultimately, can we as Christians believe that way, much though human beings living in so uncertain a climate might want to. One of the key teachings of the Bible, which is absent from Islam, is the whole notion of sin. As long as there is sin, there can surely be no true and lasting peace. As we embark on our journey of discovery, we should keep hold of that truth, however easy it is to be tempted otherwise.

The book of Hebrews teaches us that Abraham is a splendid example of faith. He is also—as the Bible, with its wonderful honesty, doesn't hide from us—someone with many human foibles and failings. As with so many characters throughout the Bible, we can easily identify with his many struggles. For Christians, he is in fact a wonderful example of precisely how we can prevail in troubled times in a world that seems mysterious and hostile where God's people are permanently under some kind of powerful, often overwhelming threat. This may not make him the ecumenical, all-things-to-all-people person beloved by the well-intentioned secular media, but he's as powerful an encouragement to twenty-first-century Christians as he has been to faithful Jews and Christians for thousands of years.

A GOD DIVIDED

Interestingly, as Paul Johnson writes in *A History of the Jews* (Weidenfeld and Nicolson, 2001), the Bible stories, from the beginning, are profoundly moral. This distinguishes them sharply from contemporary tales we see in ancient Sumerian and Babylonian tablets in which things just happen without any kind of moral commentary to go with the story. In the Bible, we see the life of Abraham and his circle and God's commentary, provided through the Holy Spirit's inspiration to the writers. This unique feature of the Old Testament, in strong distinction from contemporary Middle Eastern writings, is, to me at least, proof positive of divine inspiration.

Abraham came from what is now Iraq, a part of the world as much in the news today as it has ever been. He was of Semitic ancestry, a racial group that right down to the present day includes both Jews and Arabs and some Ethiopians (of mixed ancestry). Ur was the capital of a great, highly advanced, partially literate nation, Sumeria. Much of Ur was uncovered in twentieth-century archaeological excavations by Sir Leonard Woolley in the 1920s and later by Sir Max Mallowan, now best known as the husband of the novelist Agatha Christie. (One of her novels is set in such a dig.)

Artifacts that would have been familiar to Abraham can be seen in museums all over the world, not just the Baghdad museum that is now famous for being looted in 2003. Tablets were even discovered with the names Abram and Laban engraved on them, proving that people by such names, while not necessarily those mentioned in Genesis, certainly existed.

One interesting architectural feature of Ur was its large ziggurat. All over the world, from Ur to the famous pyramids in Egypt to the amazingly similar structures in Mexico and Central America, ancient peoples built tall, broad-based structures as an attempt to reach God (or the gods as they saw them). We see this powerfully portrayed in the biblical account of the Tower of Babel. But it seems evident from archaeology that people from Iraq to Guatemala didn't learn the lessons God taught the people of Babel by confusing and separating them into different languages. Ur was no exception.

What's special about Abraham's story—and what makes it so important—is that God reached down to him! All that laborious building, often taking decades or more, was totally unnecessary. The whole story of the Bible is that we humans cannot, ourselves, ever reach up to God because our sin and rebellion prevent it. But God in his love and mercy reaches out to us and does so through individuals who live lives of faith and obedience to him.

By launching out into the unknown desert, Abraham and his family were taking quite a step. Ur was an advanced place, with a law code and all the accoutrements of civilized living. Out there, in the wilderness, life was usually rough and dangerously unpredictable. Yet Abraham answered God's call anyway, even though he had no idea what the future would hold.

Abraham wasn't perfect, and the Bible doesn't pretend he was. For example, he lied to protect himself when he told a king that Sarah was his sister instead of his wife. He was impatient with God, siring a child by Hagar because he didn't trust in God enough to deliver the promised child via

A GOD DIVIDED

Sarah. In other words, he was fallible like us, yet at the same time he was a wonderful example of someone who put his life totally in God's hands and risked everything to follow him.

Getting Our Stories Straight

God asked Abraham to sacrifice Isaac, and just as Abraham was about to plunge in the dagger, God provided another sacrifice. Abraham had passed the test! Christians and Jews believe this story.

I remember this story came up for discussion when I was staying once at L'Abri, the legendary Swiss mountain retreat founded by Francis and Edith Schaeffer. The students there were puzzled by it, just as many others have been. "How could God have asked him to do such a horrible thing?" they wondered.

As Johnson points out in his history of the Jews, and as the Old Testament reminds us constantly, human sacrifice was endemic among the local tribes of Abraham's time. By not making human sacrifice normal—in fact, by forbidding it— the Jews were radically different from all the peoples around them. What is special about the story is that God provided another sacrifice—a wonderful advance glimpse, Francis Schaeffer has pointed out to us, of the sacrifice Jesus Christ would make on our behalf at the cross. Now that he has made the final, all-sufficient sacrifice, there's no need for any other.

The Koran, however, alters the story and puts Hagar's son, Ishmael, on the altar instead of Isaac. And this story isn't the only instance where the Koran alters things. In the Bible, Abraham is the father of God's chosen nation, Israel; in the Koran, he's one of a vast series of prophets leading up to the climactic final messenger, Muhammad. In one sense, all three faiths revere Abraham, but the *Ibrahim* of Islam (to use his Arabic name) is actually a very different figure.

If we were to look at all the Old Testament patriarchs, this chapter would be hundreds of pages long! Unfortunately, we don't have the space to do that, but we can see recurrent themes: God's complete faithfulness and total reliability, humankind's fickle nature and total dependence on God for guidance and forgiveness. We also see in the story of Joseph that God is in charge of history, determining events and helping his faithful people in whatever dire situation they find themselves.

The story of Joseph is one of the most encouraging in the Bible, as it shows how God guides us through the most difficult circumstances and brings all things together for good. It also demonstrates how God's people can be a major force for the better, even in spiritually unsympathetic climates: Joseph became ruler of Egypt without renouncing his faith and was able to make a hugely beneficial difference to the Egyptian people. Both Joseph and another heroic biblical character, Daniel, are fabulous examples of how God's people really can be salt and light (to use a New Testament metaphor), even in the most unpromising circumstances.

We don't have to become president or prime minister to be encouraged by Joseph. All of us go through hard times. We can take heart from the fact that, although things might seem pretty mysterious to us sometimes, God is still there. He hasn't forgotten us but is working out his purposes in our lives through the conditions in which we find ourselves.

The Old and New Testaments are straight narratives; the stories have a beginning, middle, and end. It's how books of all kinds are structured. It makes them easy to follow and the lessons easier to learn. The point is, the chapters (or *suras*) in the Koran are organized not by subject or story, but by *size*. So while many familiar characters appear—although with Arabic names—finding them dotted throughout the Koran isn't always easy. Indexes help, except that only the Arabic original is canonical, and any translated version is deemed inferior. So Muslims can also learn about the characters we know, but in a form more difficult to follow than the one familiar to us in the Bible.

A Historical Note

The great narratives of Moses and the exodus are some of the most exciting stories ever written—which is why even Hollywood movies have been made about them! But scholars don't always agree on what bits of the story they believe to be true. Some say Moses is a myth; others give him considerable credence. One problem we Christians face is that anti-Christian prejudice disguised as scholarship seldom gives our Scripture the benefit of the doubt. It says, "I am objective; you are biased." This shouldn't discourage us, but we need to be aware of it when we read secular histories.

Some historians have started to give far more credence to the Bible than hitherto, but the New Chronology archaeologists, as they call themselves, are on the edge of the scholarly mainstream and so are disregarded by many in the university world. (The most famous New Chronologist is David Rohl, whose books, including *A Test of Time*, have been made into major television documentaries. Rohl is by no means Christian himself but is openly sympathetic to Old Testament history.)

One problem with the New Chronology, which looks very convincing to me as an outsider, is that it involves completely recasting the chronology of hundreds of years of ancient Egyptian history. There's no innate problem with this, although many mainstream archaeologists remain skeptical. The real difficulty, however, is that cranks, New Age gurus obsessed with the pyramids, and other questionable characters also do this. This shouldn't in and of itself discredit the genuine scholarship of the New Chronology, which is very far from New Age, but it does put them in somewhat unfortunate company, especially to people who don't want to take their work seriously.

This is a shame, because in *A Test of Time* Rohl even suggests that he has found the tomb of Joseph, whom he firmly believes to be a genuine, historical character, and that the exodus really happened. All this should be good news, which is why New Chronologists are often asked to speak to Christian groups even though they deny a religious motive for their work and disagree with the supernatural parts of the Old Testament.

It should be noted that there are Christian writers who accept the Bible's historicity and firmly reject the New Chronology. The most relevant of these is Kenneth

A GOD DIVIDED

Kitchen, a British professor of Egyptology and a contributor to *The Illustrated Bible Dictionary* (IVP/Tyndale, 1998). He is the author of the article on Moses in that book and is also one of the main sparring partners, in print and on television, of Rohl and the whole New Chronology movement attempting to synchronize Bible authenticity with dating the pharaohs.

So we have to take the existence and extraordinary lives of Moses and many of the Old Testament patriarchs on faith. That shouldn't be a problem for Christians, and it could be that new discoveries will vindicate the biblical position further. Some version of the New Chronology may be accepted more widely if its attempts to synchronize Scripture with Egyptian history are proved correct.

Moses may or may not have been contemporary with Ramses II, the best known of all the pharaohs. Either way, we believe Moses led the children of Israel out of Egypt in the exciting story of the exodus.

Why Moses Was So Important

It's striking how many Christian commentaries make the same very important point: When Moses gave the Ten Commandments and the law, he wasn't just establishing a law code. He was, by God's instructions, doing something far more important: establishing a firm and binding covenant between God and the Israelites, God's people. This wasn't just a legal issue, but also a relationship between the Israelites and their God.

Muslims too believe in the importance of Moses, or *Musa*, to use the Arabic form of his name. In Islam, Musa was one of the many pre-Muhammad prophets. The Koran, like the Pentateuch, is a law code telling people how to live. But it doesn't contain the aspect of covenant, of a relationship between a God who can be known personally and his people.

Once again a well-known biblical character appears in three faiths—Jewish, Christian, and Muslim—but is seen differently in all three. To the Jews, the covenant between God and Israel is still in force, never having been replaced. To Christians, it's the old covenant, since Jesus came to fulfill it and establish a new covenant between God and humanity based on Christ's finished work on the cross. To Muslims, there is simply no covenant of any description, and that's a vital distinction between Islam and the two other so-called Abrahamic faiths.

If we look at the unfolding story of the Israelites, God is forever reminding them through the prophets and other chosen messengers of the covenant they made with God on Mount Sinai. It's at the heart of the whole Old Testament message, in the same way that the atonement, the cross, and the resurrection are central to the New Testament message. It's not just a question of a law code, however important that is. Rather, the law is a result of the covenant. God is saying, in effect, "We have a covenant relationship, and this is how you ought now to behave as a result."

For Christians, as Peter discovered on the rooftop, the ceremonial parts of the law have been abolished. But the Ten

Commandments, the moral heart of the law, are still there. So while, as Paul reminds us in his epistles, we are under grace not law, that doesn't mean the moral code has disappeared. Rather the covenant through which we are reconciled to God has changed, with Jesus having fulfilled the law on our behalf through his perfect life and taken the punishment for our sins on the cross.

Moses, therefore, introduced the framework of the covenant that lasted right up until Jesus' time more than a thousand years later.

Early History of Israel

We see early on that the Israelites still didn't get it! They had to wait forty years in the wilderness before they could even enter the Promised Land, and only a chosen few of the adults who left Egypt ever got there—and Moses was not of that select number. Mere accident of birth into a Jewish family was not enough to guarantee entrance into the Promised Land, any more than birth into a Christian family guarantees entrance into heaven today. We should always remember—nominal Christianity doesn't save us; God has only children, not grandchildren.

In short, under Joshua's brave leadership, the Israelites eventually entered the Promised Land. Once again, the Israelites didn't always understand what it meant to be God's covenant people. Many failed to realize this meant being utterly different from the tribes around them, with their many gods and morality-free lifestyle. Other nations made sacrifices to their gods, but no real element of repentance was involved, since, as Elijah later mocked, you cannot speak to idols made of wood and stone!

The Israelites then had judges instead of kings, since God was their King in the proper sense of the term. This, too, is a vital concept.

Multiple nations, each with its own set of peculiar national deities, geographically surrounded Israel. To this day, tribal peoples still have this ancient approach, and deities can change from village to village. For that matter, Hinduism (despite its New Age adherents in the West) is essentially the religion of the ethnic inhabitants of the Indian subcontinent, but they don't typically attempt to evangelize people of other ancestries. Likewise, it's rare to find people not of Japanese descent practicing the Shinto religion or Taoists who are not Chinese.

However, it's clear from the Old Testament that God was not simply the God of Israel, existing alongside Phoenician, Hittite, and Egyptian deities. Rather, the Old Testament makes it clear that he and he alone is God—there are no others. This is *monotheism*, from the Greek word meaning "one god."

Secular historians disagree on where the Jewish concept originated. Sigmund Freud, the famous twentieth-century psychologist—himself of Jewish descent—took to the theory that the Jews gained the notion from an ancient Egyptian pharaoh known to us as Akhenaten.

Akhenaten abolished all previous gods, including the main Egyptian deity, Amun, and established the worship of the sun disc, the Aten, as the sole cult in Egypt.

Here the chronological issue arises, because it's possible, according to whose reckoning is accepted as valid, that Moses long *preceded* the Aten religion and couldn't have been influenced by what came later.

Even so, the Aten religion is different because it was essentially a political religion that obliged everyone to follow and obey the pharaoh, who declared himself the only intermediary between the Egyptian people and the new god. In other words, here we are seeing a political rather than a major theological shift, since the priests of the old religion of Amun were a considerable source of rivalry to any pharaoh who wanted as much power as possible for himself. Akhenaten didn't declare all other religions of all other peoples to be false, but rather that the Aten religion was now to be the only faith over Egypt, where he wanted to be undisputed ruler.

This isn't so much monotheism as *henotheism*—the idea that each people, instead of having several gods, should worship just one god. The ancient Egyptians had many gods. The Heretical Pharaoh, as Akhenaten is sometimes called, substituted just one—the Aten. But there was still no universal concept of monotheism, suggesting that other peoples should also have to worship Aten.

So when the Israelites established that their God was the *only* one, they were innovators without any parallel in history, even from a secular point of view. From a theological perspective, it is the true God revealing himself to a chosen race, and that is how we should look at it.

Eventually the Israelites wanted a king just like all the other tribal groups around them. The first king, Saul, turned out to be a disaster. Then came a godly ruler—David, whose earthly line eventually led to *the* anointed King, Jesus himself. David was therefore a forerunner of Jesus, and that is how Christians perceive him today.

David, or *Daud* in Arabic, is also common to all three monotheistic faiths. Throughout the rest of the Old Testament, he is the king *par excellence*, someone who trusted God and ruled as a king should.

As before, archaeologists argue about whether or not David and his kingdom really existed as described in the Bible. Once more, the highly controversial New Chronology comes to the rescue of the biblical narrative. Its supporters realign the Egyptian chronology so that Saul and then David are the leaders mentioned by frightened local rulers in the famous Amarna tablets, discovered many years ago, which date from ancient Egypt.

But plenty of other archaeologists accept David and his successors as fully historical while completely rejecting New Chronology approaches. Christians accept the Old Testament's historicity in general, but we are now moving into territory where the archaeological record makes rejecting Israel's history increasingly difficult for anyone to do.

David was the great hero king; but, as the story of Bathsheba tells us, he was far from perfect. Once more, as with the patriarchs, the Bible is always honest. It also tells the moral behind the story. The prophet Nathan makes it clear to King David that he has sinned, and we read his wonderful song of repentance in the book of Psalms.

David was king, but he was not Israel's priest. Here Judaism differs from both Christianity and Islam.

In Christianity, the New Testament proclaims Jesus to be King, the king David should have been were he a perfect man, which, of course, he was not. In fact, Jesus is David's direct descendant, an heir to the throne, as it were.

Muhammad, we shall see, was the spiritual and military/political leader of the early Islamic *umma*, or community of the faithful.

However, Jesus is in heaven, not commanding armies here on earth. So where David and the Israelites divided the priestly and kingly functions, Jesus combined the two, being both our King and our High Priest. In this regard, both Christianity and Judaism differ from Islam; for in Islam (at least in the majority Sunni version) there is no priestly caste at all.

For instance, in Israel David was king, but the descendants of Levi formed a priestly group that was separate; so the secular ruler and the high priest had separated functions. Therefore it wasn't the king who would make the annual sacrifice in the temple: The priests were responsible to God, not to the king. In fact, it was their duty, if they did it properly, to confront the king if he was sinning.

The temple came into its full glory under Solomon, who, while legendarily wise, was not all he should have been. In fact, the Bible tells us that none of the kings of Israel followed the Lord and that not very many of the kings of Judah, the true Davidic line, were at all godly. The decision of the Jews to have kings like all the other tribes around was clearly unwise, just as Samuel had predicted.

It's the message of Scripture that the security of the Jewish kingdom and the obedience of the king and people to

God were permanently interwoven. If the ruler and people obeyed the Lord, they were safe. If not, God delivered them into the hands of their enemies. Faithfulness and national security went hand in hand.

Soon the kingdom of Israel ended, never to be reassembled, and that of Judah teetered on, only to fall and be captured in its turn. Until 1948, the Jews were to be under foreign rule, and increasing numbers of them exiled from their ancestral land.

But the remarkable thing, as the book of Daniel shows so clearly, is that this didn't in any way affect Judaism, the Jewish people's faith. As with Christianity in later years, being conquered, persecuted, and generally oppressed has not destroyed the Jewish faith.

In fact, one could say that the turn to twentieth-century secularism and intermarriage with non-Jews has done more to diminish the faith of the Jewish people than all the Assyrian rulers, Seleucid kings, crusader knights, and Nazi fanatics throughout history. The twentieth century has, thankfully, also seen something else—the considerable growth of Messianic Jews, who realize Jesus Christ is the Jewish Messiah—indeed, the Messiah of all who believe in him.

Daniel is a continuing example of someone whose faith stands firm despite the worst imaginable persecution. It's a lesson we will see again and again, right down to our own times—whatever humans may try to do, however terrible they are, they can do nothing to thwart God's purposes or destroy his people.

Ezra and then Nehemiah chronicle the return of many Jews to the Promised Land. (We forget that many didn't

A GOD DIVIDED

return—Mesopotamia, the land of exile, continued to be home to large numbers of Jews until the 1940s; and the New Testament shows us first-century Jews lived all over the Roman Empire as well.)

Those who returned had not forgotten the spiritual lessons of the exile. Repentance and dedication were at the heart of rebuilding the temple. Not only that, but the Jewish survivors were now under foreign rule, as they would be for well over two thousand years. The Davidic line, in the political sense, was never restored.

We now move into the intertestament period of Jewish history, the stretch of several hundred years between the end of the Old Testament and the beginning of the New. It's evident that faith continued, but so too did periods of persecution, such as that of the Seleucid ruler Antiochus Epiphanes, who profaned the temple by setting up a pagan altar there.

There were kings, but they were client kings of foreign rulers, such as Herod and his family. For a brief while during the Hasmonaean dynasty, the chief priest acted as ruler. But even then, the country really existed under sufferance, able to flourish because neither the eastward-expanding Roman Empire nor the westward-expanding Seleucid Empire was powerful enough to deny the other rule over the Holy Land.

A PEOPLE OF GOD

✡ ✝ ☪

Liberal scholars tend to date much of the Old Testament to two periods. The first is that of theological recovery under Josiah, when Judah was still an independent kingdom. Critics believe the "rediscovery" of the books of the law is when they were actually written, since they regard Mosaic authorship as impossible. The other period is when the exiles returned and Nehemiah rebuilt the temple.

To such writers, this is when what we call "Judaism" really began. Even otherwise sympathetic authors such as Paul Johnson, whose works have been read by many American Christians, deem this argument true. (Johnson, like me, is a generalist historian, writing on many different time periods, including U.S. history.)

Liberals also, almost by definition, do not believe in prophecy. If a Bible passage predicts a future event, they automatically believe it *must* have been written *after* the event occurred. A classic example of this is the book of Daniel, which the scholars claim must have been written not only after the return from exile, but even later, because it mentions the Greek rulers of the Persian Empire who weren't around until two centuries after the exiles' first return.

As Christians, we should have no problem with biblical prophecy. It's fair to say there are some Christian theologians who might, for example, see Isaiah as being written by two people rather than just by Isaiah himself. While I'd take a more conservative view, I'm no expert in ancient Hebrew. But either way, Christians of all schools agree on Isaiah's theological importance and the clear evidence that by his time Jews agreed their God really was universal in scope, with power well beyond the nation of Israel. In retrospect, we know why they developed this concept of God, with Isaiah's clear prophecy of the suffering servant fulfilled in Jesus Christ—a Savior not just for Jews but for all who would believe, including Gentiles like most of us.

Many of the groups we see in Jesus' time rose in the four-plus centuries between the return to Jerusalem and Jesus' arrival. The Sadducees stuck to the law only but tended to be aristocrat friendly and close to the Hellenistic influences we'll discover shortly. The Pharisees were the popular party, known for their piety but also for their decision to add reams of man-made legislation to God's law, as if what was written in the Torah wasn't quite enough.

A God Divided

There was also a reform party, which wanted to liberalize the Jewish faith. Like theological liberals today, they wanted to accommodate whatever was in fashion—in this instance, it was Greek, or Hellenistic, philosophy.

THE EFFECT OF HELLENISM

Why was popular, or *koine*, Greek, the *lingua franca* of Christ's time? To understand this we need to go back three hundred years to the conquests of Alexander.

Alexander the Great was one of the most successful conquerors the world has ever seen, in a very short time creating an empire that stretched from Macedonia in the Balkans (his homeland) to the borders of present-day India. In terms of sheer size, this easily matched the subsequent and far longer-lasting Roman Empire.

After Alexander died, his empire split into different parts, each ruled by the descendants of one of his generals. In Egypt this was Ptolemy, whose dynasty lasted until the time of Cleopatra, the last of her line. In the Middle East were the Seleucids, whose empire also lasted several centuries. Even today there are blond-haired, blue-eyed inhabitants of Afghanistan and the mountainous parts of Pakistan who are direct descendants of Alexander's soldiers.

The Macedonians' language was Greek. The Greek name for Greece is *Hellas*, and the new empires brought with them not only the Greek language, but also the Greek culture. This process was called *Hellenization*, and there were enormous Greek communities in the Middle East until the

1950s. In Egypt, for example, Alexandria is named after Alexander, and Iskander, as he has become known in the Middle East, is a figure of legend of whom many tales are still told.

As Paul Johnson correctly points out, much in Jewish belief and culture was well ahead of anything the Greek philosophers could have invented. Monotheism itself was a major intellectual breakthrough, even if looked at from a purely secular angle, since the Greeks believed in a whole pantheon of gods.

Nonetheless, many Jews were intellectually seduced by advanced Greek philosophy, as many Christians are, alas, by similar temptations in our own time. It should be said there was much good in Greek thinking. We gained the idea of democracy from the Greeks (*demos kratos* = people rule), and Greek mathematics, especially geometry, is of considerable use even today. Greek medicine, too, was of high quality, and doctors still take the *Hippocratic oath* to promise that they will not harm their patients. We can thank the ancient Greeks for much.

Not only that, but the popular form of Greek became *the* language of the Middle East. One could speak the same language from Sicily, where the Greeks had ancient colonies, to the Indus River and Hindu Kush and still be understood. This made an enormous difference to the spread of the gospel when Christ came. A treatise—such as the New Testament—written in Greek could be comprehended by millions of people who all spoke or understood *koine* Greek, but who also spoke a myriad of different, mutually incomprehensible languages. Rather like the invention of the

A GOD DIVIDED

printing process just before the Reformation, the wide-spread use of the Greek language in the areas where the Christian faith began proved to be providential in spreading the good news to as many different nations as possible.

But, as Paul realized several centuries later, there was something that the Greeks completely lacked. They had many gods and goddesses but no knowledge at all of the one true God.

While the Greeks did believe in a whole Mount Olympus of pagan deities, they were, in many ways, the intellectual ancestors of the nonreligious, secular thinkers of our own time. *We can do it ourselves*, they thought—much as their fifteenth-century Renaissance followers stated explicitly when the great canon of Greek literature was rediscovered in Europe.

Then, as now, many (including Jews) found this secular thinking highly seductive. Successive rulers planted large Greek colonies in the Middle East—the Decapolis of Jesus' time was named for the Greek words for "Ten Cities." There were Greeks and those born non-Greek who spread the cause of Greek culture—the Hellenizers. As Johnson points out, the Romans conquered the Greeks, but Greek culture conquered much, if not most, of the Roman Empire.

By Jesus' time, the Holy Land was no longer under either Seleucid or Ptolemaic rule. Rome had conquered the Middle East, including Egypt, following the defeat of Anthony and Cleopatra at the battle of Salamis. Part of the region was ruled indirectly through the Idumaean dynasty, founded by Herod the Great. Other parts were under direct Roman rule. But Greeks were still everywhere, and literate people and traders would all have some working knowledge of the Greek language.

THE ROOTS OF MONOTHEISM

All devout Jews were monotheists; and, although we have no canonical books from this time to tell us, one trusts some Jews surely had a living relationship with God.

While Christians believe monotheism goes back further than liberal scholars would allow, experts of all stripes call the Jewish beliefs of this time *ethical monotheism*. It wasn't just that the Jews believed in one God and that no other divine being existed. It is also that this monotheism was firmly ethical, based upon a God-given law code that had clear, well-enunciated moral standards. Compare this with the stories of the Greek and Roman gods, who were always getting in and out of scrapes, and it is easy to see an enormous ethical difference between the Jews' faith and the religions of the peoples around them.

Even secular academic scholars have recognized something unique and special about the Jews. For many years now a ferocious argument has raged in university circles on exactly when nationalism began, with no one single consensus prevailing. However, several schools of thought make the Jewish people the origins of the modern nation-state.

What is particularly fascinating is that many secular academics realize that it was the Jews' faith that made them so distinct. In particular, British sociologist Anthony Smith attributes special strength to what he calls *salvation religions*.

This theory makes enormous sense from a spiritual point of view as well. The Jews of this period were under alien domination, yet they stuck firmly to their faith and refused to blend in to their oppressors' religions. The Jewish remnant, in the Holy Land and in other parts of the Roman, Seleucid, and (later on) Parthian Empires, remained faithful to the God of their ancestors.

Many weird and strange tales have been written about the ten "lost" tribes of the northern kingdom of Israel. It's clear the Samaritans are descended from them in some way—Samaritans still exist, but in tiny numbers. By and large, it's evident that they merged into the tribes around them and that the overwhelming majority lost whatever Jewish beliefs they might have had. The Old Testament teaches there were no good kings of Israel, as opposed to Judah, and the people were sadly in the same spiritual condition.

But the remnant of Judah knew that theirs was a faith of salvation, and that is why they survived. In our own century, where do we find worshippers of Zeus, Jupiter, Baal, or Isis? All these ancient religions, once so powerful, have vanished. For that matter, no one today follows Woden or any of the Norse gods of our own ancestors. But millions of Jews remain, and Christianity is the largest single faith in today's world.

Tenacious Survival

Let us return, after that important theological parenthesis, to our narrative and see how Jews of the Holy Land coped with the increased Hellenization around them.

The Pharisees resisted, often with the support of the ordinary people, while the Sadducees and the court faction, the Herodians, were closer to the establishment, since many of the latter two groups were of high birth.

We tend, understandably, to look askance at the Pharisees in Jesus' time. But their group actually began with good intentions—to obey the law, since they knew that sin had ended the old kingdoms and driven the Jews into exile. Tragically, by Christ's time, they had lapsed into legalism. Through what became the Talmud, they added volumes of minutiae to the law, so the original became rapidly swamped by man-made legislation. This inevitably bred the kind of self-righteousness we see described in the Gospels and the idea that works can save you—the letter of the law rather than the spirit.

Another group was the Essenes. Like the later Catholic monastic orders, their reaction to the threat of Hellenism was to retreat into the desert. The Qumran community is the best known of these separatist desert groups.

Then there was the political reaction. The Maccabean revolt of 166 BC brought a brief respite from foreign domination. This continued in different formats as the oppressors changed—by Jesus' time, the main group was the Zealots, an armed resistance to Roman rule. This too failed, with the suppression of the Great Jewish Revolt and the mass suicide of the rebels at the mountain fortress of Masada in AD 72.

By the time Jesus came, the four groups had, in effect, all lost their way. Aristocratic faction, legalism, desert retreat, and political violence all were dead ends taking the Jews nowhere.

A GOD DIVIDED

Jews did, though, have one special privilege in the Roman Empire—they alone were exempt from emperor worship.

Worshipping the emperor as a god was a political act, designed to ensure the full loyalty of the peoples of the empire. The Romans didn't try to stop them from worshipping their own local gods, but in a polytheistic society, in which everyone worshipped many gods, adding one more—the Roman emperor—was, for most citizens, not very difficult.

The Jews, however, were different. They were not henotheists—worshipping only one national god—implying that if *Yahweh* was their God, then it was fine for the Romans, for example, to worship Jupiter. Rather, as we have seen, they were monotheists—there was only one God, and there was no other. Therefore, they couldn't worship any other god because they knew no other gods existed.

Thankfully for them, in God's providence, the Romans released them from the obligation to venerate the emperor as divine. This made the Jews doubly unlike anyone else in the empire—not only were they monotheists, but their exemption reinforced their distinctiveness. (It was when the Romans realized that Christianity wasn't the same religion as Judaism that Christians began to be persecuted.)

This exemption was fortunate when it came to spreading the gospel. In Acts, you'll find Paul often went first to synagogues, then to the Gentiles. Because there were so many synagogues across the Roman Empire, when Jews became Christians—when they understood Jesus was the Messiah—there was a ready-made network spread over a wide geographical area.

The fall and destruction of the rebuilt temple in AD 70 was a major disaster, and the decision by a later Roman emperor to turn the site into a pagan center still worse. The Jews nonetheless survived in the most remarkable way. Christians differ on the significance of the political and physical restoration of the state of Israel in 1948, but it's clear from Scripture, such as Paul's epistle to the Romans, that the existence of the Jewish *people* is very much in God's providence, whether in New York or Tel Aviv. Many Jews today are essentially secular; but while many are losing their Judaism through intermarriage, many Jewish groups, especially in the United States, are remaining loyal to theologically conservative forms of the Jewish faith. (We will look at this in more depth in another chapter.)

A Savior among Us

✡   ✝   ☪

Christianity is the second of the great monotheistic faiths that look to Abraham as an inspiration. But it's also completely different from the other two.

This chapter will decidedly lean toward the Christian point of view and its claim for objective truth. But of course such an approach is incorrect from many a secular, scholarly point of view. Nor does it conform to the current fashion for post-modernism in universities and the mind-set countless Western people have adopted today. That's not to say, however, that Christianity represents the true faith for some, while Judaism or Islam might be true for others.

However, if people therefore want a more "objective" work that looks at Jesus, who he is and what he came to do, then that says something about them and their religious perspective. If all religions are equal, then, by definition, they do not believe their own philosophy, since each religion claims to be the sole objective truth! The truth claims of Islam and Christianity, the two monotheistic faiths that proclaim universal validity, are mutually contradictory. Either only one of them is true and the other is not, or neither is true. It's not possible to have two compatible claims for sole universal truth![†]

So let us proceed on that basis.

WHY IS CHRISTIANITY DIFFERENT?

We'll first look at Christianity in and of itself and then look at how it differs from what went before in Judaism and what came later in Islam. The chapter on the Muslim faith will look at some of the latter issues in more detail. But in this chapter I'll show that, while Christianity and Judaism have so much in common, secular writers eventually call Christianity and Islam the two *universal faiths*. By this they mean beliefs that claim not merely to be unique, but also applicable and open to all, regardless of race. While there have always been Gentile proselytes to the Jewish faith, by

---

[†] What follows is an approach from an explicitly Christian viewpoint. I've written belief-neutral books—before beginning this one, I finished *A Brief History of the Middle East* for two secular publishers—but this book, by its very title, *A God Divided*, aims to be objective by a different, theological standard, making clear which of the three so-called Abrahamic faiths is in fact true.

A GOD DIVIDED

and large Judaism has remained an ethnic religion. That is not true of either Christianity or Islam, and that's something that's becoming increasingly vital to remember in our global, post-9/11 age.

The Christian faith was founded in the first century AD. We don't know exactly when Jesus was born, since AD and BC ("before Christ") were put together by a monk centuries after the birth of Christianity. But it's obvious from the Gospels roughly when Jesus came to earth, since the Bible gives details of the rulers at the time. So, while AD 1 is unlikely, it's probable Christ wasn't born much earlier.

Christianity is the one monotheistic faith named after its founder, Jesus Christ. Judaism is named after a people, the Jews. *Islam* means "submission" in Arabic and is therefore a theological term—to call that faith Mohammedanism, as we used to in the West, is quite wrong.

The link between Christ and Christianity is all-important. It's what makes the Christian religion unique. It's a faith about a person, not primarily about rules on how to live. Christians believe they are saved through what Jesus *did*, not just through what he said. It's a faith about reconciliation with God through what Jesus accomplished for humanity, rather than about following a particular ethical code.

We need to emphasize this point from the very start. As we saw, the Jews had their great spiritual and national leaders. Likewise, Muhammad was a spiritual, political, and military leader rolled into one. But Jews are not saved through Abraham, nor are Muslims saved through Muhammad himself, however much they revere Islam's founder. Only Christians make the founder of their faith pivotal to what they believe.[†]

Christians believe that Jesus is divine—that he is God; in his case, God the Son. This in itself distinguishes Christianity from both Judaism and Islam. Jews don't hold to the divinity of any of their great heroic figures, from Abraham through Moses to David. Likewise, although Islam proclaims Muhammad to be God's final prophet, the Koran itself mentions Muhammad hardly at all, and Islam strongly rejects the idea that Muhammad is divine, however revered he might be.

The doctrine of the Trinity—three persons in one Godhead—is unique to Christianity. Both Judaism and Islam strongly teach the oneness of God; and, while we can see shadows of the Trinity in the Old Testament, neither Jews nor Muslims adhere to that doctrine. Muslims consider the concept of the Trinity blasphemous and, furthermore, even substitute Mary for the Holy Spirit.

Second, in Judaism and Islam, one is saved through obedience to the law, more so in the latter than in the former. One is also, in effect, born into the religion, although, as the Old Testament makes abundantly clear, being born Jewish does not by itself ever save anyone.

Jesus said he had come to fulfill the law, and the Bible makes it plain that the law, while intended to bring people to God, is impossible to keep in its entirety. It condemns, but it cannot save.

---

† Later, we'll consider the issue many postmodern people raise today: Is the God of the three "Abrahamic" monotheistic faiths one and the same?

A GOD DIVIDED

Judaism, as we see from the Pharisees' well-meant but often sad attempts, evolved into an increasingly legalistic religion with added laws and commandments that went far beyond Scripture's simpler, more straightforward commands. Keeping the law is one thing, and legalism another. The latter involves a mental framework that concentrates so much on the minutiae that the original spirit behind the law is lost.

Islam is yet more legalistic, certainly in its nonmystic forms. (One group of Muslims called Sufis would disagree with this premise, but many other Muslims would cast equal doubt on the Sufi interpretation of Islam.)

Also, the concept of knowing God personally is alien to Islam, certainly for ordinary Muslims. While Christians say it's ultimately through Jesus Christ that people can truly know God, it's nonetheless clear it was very possible to have a relationship with God in Old Testament times. One only has to examine the prayer lives of great Jewish leaders such as Abraham, Moses, David, Daniel, and Nehemiah to see that this is true. While later Jewish ritual became increasingly formulaic, and thus impersonal, the Old Testament still relays a very powerful sense of individuals having real relationships with God.

Outside of some of the more mystical Sufi brotherhoods, there's no real sense of such an intimate relationship with God in Islamic history. Writers such as Bernard Lewis and John Esposito have explained Sufism as an attempt to have a more personal faith in light of Koranic Islam's impersonal, law-based nature. Significantly, this is in many ways precisely the objection that mainstream Islam has to Sufi thought; it is considered syncretistic, as it seems to borrow from medieval Christian monasticism and perhaps from central Asian Buddhism as well.

But in both Judaism and Islam, no one is saved through a person. It is one's own righteous deeds and adherence to the law that get one into heaven.

Christianity is thus completely different. It is, like Judaism and Islam, a faith of revelation, of God's proclaiming his message to humanity. But in contrast with Judaism, in Christianity God's revelation is now complete. In contrast to Islam, the revelation is a person, not a law code.

Many of us who grew up as Christians were taught when we were younger that only Christianity was a religion of revelation. Strictly speaking, this isn't true, since Judaism and Islam are as well. But only the Christian revelation is the truly complete revelation of the character and personality that is God, and that revelation is quite unlike that of the other two religions. The distinction is much like comparing a media representation of a government official to that of the government official's spouse. Which one really knows the official?

Jews weren't saved through Abraham, nor are Muslims saved through what Muhammad did while alive. Christians are saved entirely and solely through Jesus Christ. Human righteousness, as Isaiah knew, is like filthy rags—even the most righteous of people cannot save themselves.

This is why the doctrine of grace is so important. It's the distinguishing feature of the Christian faith, though it is implicitly there in the Old Testament, since it's clear that simply being Jewish was not enough for salvation. The godly Jews, as the book of Hebrews reminds us, were saved through a faith relationship with the personal God, even as

A GOD DIVIDED

Christians are; the real difference is that Christians now know how and through whom they are saved.

In Britain, as in the United States, the Christmas holiday has for all intents and purposes become the secular feast of Xmas. Nevertheless, Jesus' birth narrative is very special and again unique—we know about the adult lives of Abraham and Muhammad but no details of their births. Jesus' advent was no ordinary event, and it's important that Christians keep emphasizing the miraculous nature of the faith. The virgin birth is one of the most important of such miracles. Jesus' birth, which was originally celebrated on a pagan midwinter festival (and which almost certainly did not occur on December 25) that the early church abolished and then took over, really is the unique event of God's coming to earth in human form. Only Christianity offers this unique element: a Savior who was tempted in all points as we humans are, but, unlike us, never sinned.

Spiritually, it's in some ways strange that we celebrate Christmas out of proportion to Easter. Christmas happened in order that Easter could take place. The heart of the Christian message is what Christ did in dying for us on the cross, taking the punishment for our sins, then rising again on the third day.

The concept of the atonement, of a sacrificial offering for sin, is also highly visible in the Old Testament. However, the sacrifice needed repeating, since once was never enough. Christ's death on the cross is the once and for all, eternally adequate sacrifice that never needs repetition.

Atonement and redemption are completely unknown in Islam, which therefore differs altogether from Christianity and Judaism. This, as stressed by the many evangelistic books for Christians to use in witnessing to Muslim friends, is one of Christianity's key distinctive features. Not only can people know God personally, but God has taken the initiative to redeem all those who turn to him in repentance and faith.

The Gospels are Jesus' life story, and here they differ again from the Old Testament and the Koran. The New Testament states that Jesus was without sin; and the Old Testament, as we saw, is refreshingly honest about the ups and downs of some of its leading characters. (The New Testament doesn't hide the disciples' human foibles, which also makes it different from the Koran, but the gospel narrative isn't focused on them.) In the Koran, there's effectively no mention of Muhammad at all. While the *sunnah*, or life, of Muhammad is important, the sources for his biography are not within the Koran.

THE CENTRAL PLACE OF SCRIPTURE

Muslims refer to Jews and Christians as "people of the Book"—the book in question being the Koran. As a result, Jews and Christians have special status within Islam. In a sense, all three faiths are book centered. Protestant and evangelical Christians in particular set huge store by the Bible and its importance in the doctrine of *sola scriptura* (Scripture alone). As someone who believes deeply in the infallibility and inerrancy of Scripture, I would be the first to defend the Bible's centrality in all that we Christians

A GOD DIVIDED

think or do! We know what we know about who God is and what he has done by what we read in the pages of the Old and New Testaments. The teaching of Scripture is the yardstick against which we judge all doctrine and lifestyles. In that sense, we are very similar both to Jews, with whom we share the Old Testament, and to Muslims, to whom the Koran is central.

However, in one sense the Old and New Testaments subtly diverge from the Koran. All three books contain laws, a mandate on how to live a righteous life. The Old Testament contains an enormous amount of law code. For example, there is a wonderful account in the books of Second Kings and Second Chronicles in which King Josiah leads the people of Judah to rediscover God's Word. While the New Testament doesn't have a direct equivalent of the Pentateuch, there's plenty there on a godly lifestyle.

We can also say that both Hebrew and Christian Scriptures are about a relationship of God with his people. We see the story of people who knew God unfolding through the Old Testament pages. In both the Old and New Testaments, we have a marriage analogy: the children of Israel, the faithful of the kingdom of Judah, and then the church itself are all seen as a bride married to a faithful husband.

This analogy is unique to the Bible. The faithful Jews were God's old-covenant people, as true believers in the church are in Jesus Christ's new covenant. What once was restricted to one nation is now possible for anyone in any race or country.

The nearest that Islam gets is the concept of the *umma*, or faithful people of Allah. Here we get the concept alluded to earlier of Christianity and Islam being the two "universalisms."

A FAITH FOR EVERYBODY

This idea of universal faiths is more a political science concept than a theological one. We need to look at it as responsible citizens of our own countries, as it's at the heart of much public and international debate, especially since 9/11.

Let us start where all Christians should always begin: with the Bible.

In the book of Acts, we see Christianity rapidly becoming a multinational, multicultural faith, with people from all over the Roman Empire and beyond becoming Christians, including Gentiles with no previous Jewish connections. Soon a man from a hitherto banned group—eunuchs—is converted, and he is from Ethiopia, an African country outside Roman jurisdiction, at that. Later, Peter discovers that the early Jewish dietary laws no longer apply to Gentile Christians, and even hated Roman occupiers are welcome within the church.

In a very short time, the gospel spreads everywhere, despite being illegal since Christians refused to worship the emperor as divine.

In theory, Islam began in a similar way—as a faith of Arabs, which then spread thousands of miles in both directions, from Spain to Iran. The Islamic community, or *umma*, is, like the church, now global, multiracial, and made up of people from all classes of society.

If we look at some of the other major religions, we see they're often still highly ethnic. Though some more free-spirited Westerners have embraced Eastern religions, Hinduism remains largely the religion of India and of Indians now living in other parts of the world, such as Britain or the United States. The same applies to Buddhism—there are a few Western Buddhist converts, especially among disciples of the Tibetan Dalai Lama. But in general, neither Hinduism nor Buddhism is active in evangelism or makes the kind of universal claims to exclusive truth common to Christianity and Islam. Judaism, by definition, is the faith of the Jewish people, and the few proselytes today are usually Gentiles who marry into a family of believing Jews.

One of the most well-known international-relations theories of recent years is that of Harvard professor Samuel P. Huntington, called the *clash of civilizations* after an article he wrote in 1993 and a book he published under the same title in 1996. One of his main theses stated that, after the American-Soviet clash of the cold war, religion would become a major player in future conflicts. In par-ticular, he believed that Islam had "bloody borders" and that a clash between the Islamic world and the Christian West was one day inevitable. Come 9/11, he and many others believed this theory had come true.

Osama bin Laden clearly also believes in this theory in a modified way. Bin Laden contrasts the world of belief, the *dar al-Islam*, with that of unbelief, the *dar al-harb*, led by the crusader-minded United States.

Some writers and thinkers, including distinguished Christian human-rights activist and intellectual Paul Marshall, give Huntington much credence. After 9/11 and the similar subsequent attacks in Madrid and London, it's easy to see why.

However, many also disagree profoundly with the whole clash of civilizations thesis from many different points of view. I'll try to examine it from a biblical angle.

Islam, as we'll see in more detail later, fuses church and state. Bin Laden and others see the whole Islamic world—the *umma*—as one giant Muslim superstate. One of their explicit aims is to restore the *caliphate*, the great Islamic empire that lasted in various forms from the seventh century to the demise of the Ottoman Empire in the twentieth century. Bin Laden refers to Muslim people as one monolithic bloc and also to Westerners as a similar monolithic, non-Islamic entity.

Politically, there are problems with this concept. According to the theory, all the Catholic and Protestant West, essentially western/central Europe and the Americas, are part of the Christian West. (Huntington and others separate countries that are Orthodox, such as Russia, although today several Orthodox countries, such as Greece, are within the European Union.) But do we really think the United States and France are the same? On a cultural and political level, let alone anything else, French people and Americans would have a few things to say about that!

There's also the problem of what sociologists call the *secularization theory*. In the past, secular (and often militantly anti-Christian) sociologists would proclaim that as the world grew more sophisticated and modern, religion would decline correspondingly, especially in the advanced countries of the West.

Now, however, these experts are eating their words! It's obvious—even to academics living in secular cocoons—that the world, if anything, is becoming *more* religious, not less! Not only that, but the religion that is spreading the most by far is Christianity, the faith the sociologists said would soon be in terminal decline.[†]

It seems the only exception to this is Western Europe. There, nominal Christianity is in very sharp decline, and large areas of Europe have far fewer Christians living in them than many parts of Africa. Several global missions organizations are now saying, correctly, that with the rapid growth of Christianity in the two-thirds world, Europe now needs the missionaries. In Britain, we now have missionaries and mission-planted churches from places as far afield as Nigeria and Brazil, and these are often some of the most vibrant churches around. The part of Britain where I live, East Anglia, has thankfully retained its Puritan roots, so now that famous university city of Cambridge is nicknamed Britain's Bible Belt! But it is, sadly, an exception to the Western European rule of Christian decline.

This means large parts of the so-called Christian West are now anything but, being mainly secular and decidedly

---

[†] In all fairness, Christianity is also enjoying rapid growth on secular Western campuses—and among academics, not just students. Many of Cambridge's most eminent scientists are or have been evangelicals, and I was more than pleasantly surprised to see how many evangelicals were on the faculty of the University of Virginia when I was there in 2001.

post-Christian. By contrast, parts of Africa, Central America, and Asia (such as Singapore and Korea) now have enormous, growing, and active Protestant Christian churches. Only the United States fits the pattern of the "Christian West," and while the vibrancy of American evangelicalism is impressive, many evangelicals in the United States take a gloomier perspective![†] They argue it's very hard to view a country with an abortion rate as high as that of the United States as a Christian country.

While I would want to defend the liveliness of American evangelicals (not just because I married one), I do see the pessimists' point. As I have argued in *Whose Side Is God On?* (Church Publishing, 2003), it is God's people who constitute the church, not any particular nation. Lots of wonderful Christian people live in the United States, but in the strict biblical sense we cannot call it a Christian country in the same way Muslims would describe Saudi Arabia as an Islamic state.

In other words, while Bin Laden and his kind merge all Muslims into a single political-spiritual entity, we can't do the same for the West. As Christians, our spiritual allegiance is to the kingdom of heaven. In the West, there is thankfully little conflict of interest between submitting to Christ and

---

[†] Use of the term *evangelical* in this book should always be understood not in its often popular political connotations, but rather in its ancient theological sense. Evangelicals are those who affirm that the Bible is the truthful revelation of God, the Creator of all that exists; that God has entered history redemptively in the incarnation of Jesus Christ, fully God and fully man; that God's nature exists in Trinitarian form; and that Jesus Christ will return at the consummation of human history to bring about resurrection and final judgment.

A GOD DIVIDED

submitting to the government of the country in which we live.

However, for many Christians, especially those living in unsympathetic nations, such as Pakistan or China, things are completely different and are much more analogous to the early church's situation in the Roman Empire.[†]

We might be able to combine being patriotic Britons or Americans and active Christians; but in much of the world, especially where the church is growing the fastest, Christians have to choose whether or not to put loyalty to country above obedience to God. If they choose the latter, they suffer accordingly.

While to Muslims, the *dar al-Islam* and the *dar al-harb* are political as well as spiritual concepts, Christians always need to separate the two. Any theory, therefore, that posits a "Christian" West against an "Islamic" East is highly problematic from a theological point of view, especially since the church is now become stronger in non-Western countries.

However, this isn't surprising. An important theme in this book is that Islam is a religion of *power*. By this I mean it presupposes a Muslim ruler over either an equally Islamic nation or "people of the Book" who have to pay (literally, in the form of higher taxes) a price for their rejection of Islam.

However, there *is* a clash in another sense, and this theory is described by a Muslim academic who teaches at

---

[†] Even as I write this, I've just read an article—in a secular newspaper—by a British Christian leader bemoaning the burning to the ground of yet another Christian church in Pakistan.

a German university: Bassam Tibi, author of *The Challenge of Fundamentalism: Political Islam and the New World Disorder*. He refers to the *clash of universalisms*, in particular the two faiths that claim universal truth: Christianity and Islam.

THE RIVALRY BETWEEN CHRISTIANITY AND ISLAM

As we've seen, there's not a Christian equivalent to the Muslim world. The West is now increasingly secular, and Christians frequently inhabit countries in which they are persecuted minorities. It's hard-line Muslim groups such as al-Qaeda that see a *political* clash between the *dar al-Islam* and the West.

There is, however, a spiritual truth behind all this, because Islam often competes for converts in the same areas where the church is growing. Looking at matters theologically, this is surely no coincidence. In many parts of the world, people's eyes are blinded by materialism and an entirely secular, self-centered worldview. Modernity in such places is often the enemy of the church.

However, in most of the world ordinary people are still innately religious. They are, though, increasingly rejecting the paganism and superstition of their ancestors. In some places they are turning to faith in Jesus Christ in large numbers. But in other regions they're responding to the siren call of Islam. In many places, these areas overlap geographically. Some of the most violent clashes in the world today are along these

A GOD DIVIDED

fault lines—to use Huntington's expression—in countries such as Nigeria and Indonesia. In Nigeria, for example, Christianity is spreading from the coast upward, through the center, to the north. Islam, which came over the Sahara Desert some centuries ago, is spreading southward. Needless to say, some of the worst riots in which Christians are killed are in central Nigeria.

Often the vicious clashes come in the Nigerian states (the country is divided similarly to the United States) where a Muslim majority wishes to impose specifically Islamic, or *sharia*, law. (We will look at this more closely in the chapter on Islam.) This disadvantages Christians and all other non-Muslims considerably. There have been major riots and non-Muslims condemned to death.

It's fair to say here that all this horrifies some moderate Muslims! While the president of Iran in power as I write this is regarded as an Islamic extremist—possibly even more extreme than many of the ayatollahs—a former Iranian president, Mohammad Khatami, rejected an oppressive and violent approach. When he was in power, he tried—often in vain—to liberalize the country. But he did succeed in considerably extending women's rights. Khatami believed zealously in what he called the *dialogue of civilizations*, which meant people of different faiths talking to one another without violence. His followers even staged *pro-American* demonstrations after 9/11; and a brave group of women in Tehran, the capital, started doing their daily aerobics to "The Stars and Stripes Forever" just to show their solidarity!

On many moral issues, such as abortion, Muslims are on the same side as Christians. In Britain, local Islamic *imams* (Muslim leaders) and Christian pro-life campaigners often find common cause. Francis Schaeffer called this *co-belligerency*, and we can be grateful that on many such matters, Christians are not fighting alone against our society's increasing decadence.

Similarly, when a British Baptist peace activist was kidnapped in Iraq in 2005, British Muslims, horrified at those who would give Islam a bad reputation in the West, leaped to his defense, demanding his release on Arabic satellite TV network Al Jazeera. Because one group of devout Muslims was speaking to another, it had the credibility that Western diplomats lacked.

However, looking at things globally, one can say that Islam is as much a spiritual rival to Christian faith throughout the world as materialism is in the West. Jesus said, "I am the way, the truth, and the life. No one comes to the Father except through Me" (John 14:6). That's a universal truth claim if ever there was one, and it is a claim believed by Christians from Lagos to Manhattan. Muslims, however, believe Muhammad alone was the final prophet of God, and that too is a claim to universal exclusivity. We're so used to postmodern mush in the West that we forget that plenty of others out there also believe, as do Christians, in concepts of absolute truth. No group embodies that as much as the Muslims.

So there is a clash in the world, but it's not a political one with Saudi Arabia, Iraq, and Iran on one side and Britain, the United States, and France on the other. It's a clash between those who know that Christianity alone is the one true faith and those who proclaim that their alternative alone is true.

A GOD DIVIDED

In our Western world, consumer greed may blind the eyes of the many to the truth, but in much of the world, Islam is that rival to absolute truth.

Here Christians have a strong advantage.

One key recurrent feature of the New Testament is the ever-present reality of persecution. Again, we in the West often forget this, since the worst we usually face is social ostracism or mocking attitudes. But for much of the church today, in regions where Christians are oppressed, persecution is very similar to what the early church experienced.

Does this hinder Christian growth? The answer, from the book of Acts onward to the present, is a resounding no! Scripture's clear message is that God is in charge, however powerful the enemy on the ground may seem. Satan will be defeated, and Christ will return and triumph. Mere people cannot prevent the growth of the gospel; and, as in the first-century Roman Empire and twentieth-century China, the steadfastness of Christians under persecution often causes more conversions rather than fewer.

However, the Koran presupposes an Islamic regime is in power, which is why the situation of the millions of Muslims in Western countries today is so problematic for the Islamic faith. Only in the past few decades have Muslims actually been persecuted for their faith, often at the hands not of Christians but of extremist mobs in countries such as India, where ultranationalist Hindus have slain innocent Muslims and Christians alike.

This has led to radically different histories for the three faiths. Christians and especially Jews have historically been persecuted.

However, in both cases, the relationship with God is a personal one, based on faith and grace, not where one lives. While the Old Testament doesn't spell it out, it's clear Jews had individual relationships with God, as Christians do, and to those faithful followers corporate identity *as a geographical nation* was not the most important factor. Faithful Jews could be anywhere and still have a loving relationship with God through faith.[†]

Liberals accuse evangelicals of bibliolatry and say that, unlike us, they base their faith on Jesus, not the Bible. This naturally begs the question of how they know about Jesus, except through what Scripture teaches! If they really do believe in Jesus, there's the awkward fact that he believed totally in Scripture himself.

The Bible, Christians must understand, is God speaking to us. It's surely all the more special because it came to us over hundreds of years with many different authors, in often widely diverging literary genres—unlike the Koran, which came through just one individual in a comparatively short time. In the Bible, we see an exciting and unfolding narrative, culminating in Jesus' life and the experience of the early church.

So, the Bible is both the infallible, Holy Spirit–inspired word from God to humanity and a book written by humans for the benefit of other humans. Here it contrasts with the

---

[†] I'm avoiding the issue, deeply controversial among Christians, of whether or not the political/geographical state of Israel is part of God's plan. This book is about comparative religious truth and thus includes Jews living in all parts of the world, such as the enormous and very special Jewish diaspora in the United States.

A GOD DIVIDED

Koran, which Muslims believe was delivered verbatim to Muhammad and, as he was supposedly illiterate, then written down by his followers after his death.

Therefore, if any group could be said to be bibliolaters, it is the Muslims. They insist, for example, that only the original Arabic version of the Koran counts—unlike Christians who, especially since the Reformation, have been keen to translate the Bible into the languages of the people so that they can understand it better for themselves.

Muslims, it should be said, would reject the charge as much as Christians do, and it's fair to say that they have a good case. All the same, the Koran is impersonal in a way the Bible is not.

THE THIRD
MONOTHEISTIC FAITH

✡   ✝   ☪

I slam, founded by Muhammad in the seventh century, is the youngest of the three monotheistic, "Abrahamic" religions born in the Middle East.

One of the most important things to remember when talking to Muslims is they don't regard their faith as younger. To them, Muhammad is God's final messenger; and, far from founding a new faith, he revealed God's true message, thereby correcting the interpretation made by Jews and Christians over the centuries.

It's also important not to make the mistake committed by many Westerners in the past by calling the religion *Mohammedanism*. To Muslims, Muhammad was the final prophet but certainly wasn't divine, as Christians know Jesus to be; and naming the religion after the prophet is to perpetrate an entirely false notion of the Muslim faith's origins.

EARLY HISTORY OF ISLAM

Until comparatively recently, Muslims have endured little controversy about their faith's historicity. While critics have long poured scorn upon the authenticity of the Old and New Testaments—some Israeli archaeologists, for example, doubt David's and Solomon's genuine existence every bit as much as liberal Western theologians—Islam has somehow managed to escape. Critics of Christianity such as former nun Karen Armstrong give Islam leeway they would never give to the faith they used to know but now reject.

In recent years, however, there has been a major shift, with some Western academics now applying the same degree of criticism and doubt to Islamic origins that they've applied to Judaism and Christianity. Michael Cook at Princeton and the Cambridge-based writer Patricia Crone have now cast doubt upon the Muslim version of the dawn of Islam.

Two very different constituencies have adopted this view of early Islam. The first is the neoconservative right in the United States. Regnery, its publisher of choice, has brought out *The Politically Incorrect Guide to Islam (and the Crusades)*, which both attacks the Muslim faith and aims to justify the Crusades. Likewise, Christian human-rights groups, keen to protect the freedom of worship of fellow believers in the

Muslim world, many of whom are being persecuted, also doubt the historicity of the infant Islamic faith.[†]

As Cook points out, early, primary-source materials that can verify Islamic claims to historical authenticity are very few, almost nonexistent. There are nowhere near as many early edition copies of the Koran as of the earliest editions of the Christian Gospels. Crone, similarly, makes a strong case that infant Islam actually was much nearer to an unusual Arabic version of Judaism than to the independent, very different faith we know today. What we have, in effect, is developed Islam from later centuries read back into the origins, and the story has changed to fit.

Needless to say, Muslims of all stripes would reject such views utterly. With an infinitesimally small number of exceptions, there are simply not as many theologically liberal scholars in Islamic universities as one finds in many Western or Israeli ones. To some extent this could be prudence—such overt heresy might result in death or similar dangers, as with dissident Egyptian writer Mahfouz.

However, one group of Islamic theologians is very aware of Western liberal scholarship—but these Muslim scholars are some of the most passionate defenders of Islam and a literal reading of the Koran! It's not their faith they're attacking, but ours!

[†] I could have been wrong in some of my other books for following early academic trends and accepting, for instance, that Muhammad really was born in 570 according to tradition. A leading South Asian Christian, active in defending Christian freedom in Muslim lands, criticized me for this. I might concede now that my critic and eminent academics such as Cook and Crone are right.

So perhaps Muhammad was born in 560, 568, or 574 (take your pick) and not 570. But I do wonder whether or not we Christians are doing the right thing in allying ourselves with those who cast doubt on the factual origins of *all* three monotheistic faiths, ours included. After all, we dislike it when someone claims Christ was a mere man, never performed a miracle, certainly didn't rise from the dead, thought of himself as a mere peace-loving and reforming rabbi, and never said most of what the Bible attributes to him. We would surely also want to defend theologically conservative Jews who believe strongly in the literal existence of Moses, David, Solomon, and other parts of the Hebrew Scriptures. So why ally ourselves with those who say our history is wrong simply because they cast the same degree of doubt upon the origins of Islam?

Surely the important disagreement is the spiritual one. Even if Muhammad did receive revelations in 610, it was not God from whom they came. Whether Muhammad was forty or thirty-nine when he heard them is irrelevant compared to the fact that what he proclaimed is inconsistent with what Jews and Christians have known for millennia; and therefore, he is sadly mistaken.

In any case, the *sunnah*, or life of Muhammad, contrasts strongly with that of Jesus Christ. Even giving Muhammad the benefit of the doubt—for example, in his many marriages and the age of some of his brides—doesn't really alter the perspective very much. (Also, insulting him doesn't help much in evangelism with Muslims living in the West! We want them to listen to us, not close their minds before we have proclaimed the gospel's liberating power. Tact is surely a better witness than vitriol.)

Therefore, we need to remain open-minded about the historicity of early Islam, including Muhammad's life, on the grounds that—while much cannot be proved—nothing important is gained either way in denying or affirming it. What matters is the truth or otherwise of what he actually said and taught and the contrast between his life and Jesus' life.

Even some of the most ultraliberal Western writers would affirm that the distinction between Christianity and Islam is enormous, however politically incorrect it might be to say so. On this issue, interestingly enough, the political right has no monopoly on political incorrectness. An eminent and distinctly nonevangelical academic, after reading the Koran for the first time, said to me one only has to contrast it to, say, the Sermon on the Mount, to see a very clear difference.

Muhammad, according to tradition, was born in the Arabian Peninsula in 570 into a distinguished tribe, the Quraysh, and an eminent part of it, the Hashemites. The family is still famous to this day; King Abdullah II of the Hashemite kingdom of Jordan is a forty-third-generation direct descendant of Muhammad.

In AD 610, when he was forty, Muhammad began to have what he regarded as direct revelations from God. These form the basis of the Muslim holy book, the Koran. They came via the angel Jabril (Gabriel to us), starting with the word *recite!*

Muhammad initially gained only a few followers. Twelve years after he began his visions, in 622, he was obliged to flee from Mecca, his home city, to the nearby city of Yathrib (now called Medina). Muslims date their calendar from this flight, or *Hegira* (AH = *anno Hegirae*, year of the flight).

In Medina, he was able to raise a group of followers who became the early community of the faithful, or *umma*. His senior disciples were soon called the companions of the prophet and had special status.

A historian once described Muhammad as Jesus and Charlemagne (the sixth-century Holy Roman Emperor) rolled into one. Here we begin to see major differences between our Bible and the Koran, the holy book of Islam.

In the Old Testament, the only people who were spiritual and military leaders were Moses, Joshua, and Samuel. Abraham was a nomad, and while much Scripture is written about him, he didn't compose any himself. King David was Israel's military and political leader; but, as we see from the strong rebuke given him by the prophet Nathan, he wasn't the country's spiritual head. Instead, this job was given to the priesthood and people specially anointed to the task by God. In fact, we notice the military and spiritual functions were kept very separate for most of the Old Testament. It was the prophets who spoke God's word to the people; the occasional godly ruler, such as Josiah, used Scripture and not his own authority as the basis of righteous living. The king never made the sacrifices on the part of the people. Indeed, as we see in 1 Samuel 8, the very idea of a king represented a rejection of God himself (v. 7), yet they still preferred to be the same as all the pagan nations around them (vv. 19–20).

By the time we get to the New Testament, we notice an even greater division between the sacred governance of the temple priesthood and the secular rule of Rome and, orally, Herod.

THE ISLAMIC HOLY BOOK: THE KORAN

According to Muslim lore, Muhammad was illiterate. However, the Koran is written in the very best classical Arabic. The Islamic belief is that Muhammad received the words directly from God via Gabriel and that they were put together by the faithful after Muhammad's death. One of the most fought-over theological disputes in early Islam was whether the Koran has always existed since eternity, along with God himself, or whether it was specifically created at a point in time.

However, even the most conservative Muslim scholars agree that much of the Koran reflects the events of the life of Muhammad himself. Some parts, according to the exegetes, were composed when he was in Medina, others when he had managed to win control of Mecca. Working out exactly what was written when is guesswork, but it's of more academic than practical interest, since Muslims also believe the Koran preexisted in heaven before being revealed to Muhammad.

Even devout scholars such as Akbar Ahmed feel that the best Koranic criticism is by Muslims outside of the Islamic world, since they can write with much greater liberty than those inside it. However, since Ahmed himself believes the Koran to be completely true, he would not agree with Western scholars such as Crone and Cook who think it possible the

Koran was really written many decades after Muhammad's death. One leading scholar from the Muslim world has written similar thoughts: Ibn Warraq's work has cast doubt upon much of the Koran. It's perhaps significant that he uses a pseudonym to hide his real identity.

Having said earlier it might be unwise to sympathize with liberal critics of the Koran since many Islamic scholars happily quote liberal Western critics of the Bible to attack Christianity, we won't pursue this line further here. However, even if everything came to Muhammad over a short time span, Christians would still regard the Bible as God's final, inspired, and authoritative Word. We should not concede that any other book can ever replace it. If one reads the Koran, it's abundantly clear it's radically different from both the Hebrew Scriptures/Old Testament and the New Testament.

Muslims believe that Muhammad was illiterate and that he repeated what God had said directly to him to his followers orally. As we know little of Muhammad's actual life, it's hard to know if this is true, and maybe it doesn't matter either way.

In fact, since Muslims believe loyal followers assembled the Koran after the prophet's death, the story could well be true. The early companions of the prophet who were literate would have written down what he said and collected it all when he was no longer around to speak to them directly.

There's also a sense in which the Koran is a book made by a committee: It's organized by size, not theme, with the larger *suras* coming first and the shorter ones later. (This is one reason why it's impossible to tell in what order parts of

A GOD DIVIDED

it were written—size doesn't indicate date.) Consequently, themes appear and disappear, and the helpful thematic indexes in Western translations aren't considered proper in the Muslim world.

In addition, only the original Arabic version is regarded as lawful—only recently have translations been acceptable at all—and many Muslims still regard them with suspicion. As most Arabs do not speak the highly esteemed classical Arabic of the Koran—any more than we speak the language of Shakespeare—the majority of Arabs don't fully comprehend the Koran's language. More important still, we tend to forget that most Muslims today are *not* Arabic, but come from places such as Malaysia, Indonesia, Pakistan, and other Asian countries. For them, the Koran is in a completely foreign language and a script most of them don't use. It's as if we could only read the New Testament in its original Greek!

In the centuries since the Reformation, the situation has been radically different in the Christian world; Christians now regard it as essential that all people be able to read God's Word in *their own language*.[†] Most Catholics also now use translations, such as the Jerusalem Bible, even if they reject the Reformation doctrine of *sola scriptura*.

Western scholars now think Muhammad would have heard the Old Testament through the many Jewish merchants and traders living in the Arabian Peninsula, including Medina

---

[†] As I write this, a member of my church with Wycliffe Bible Translators has visited us on furlough. She will return to begin language work on translating the Scriptures into some of the obscure dialects of far-eastern Siberia—even the smallest linguistic groups need the Bible in their own speech!

itself. They have speculated it's possible he would have heard some unusual version of Christian doctrine through the strong links between Arabia on one side of the Red Sea and Ethiopia on the other. The Ethiopian church was influenced by many heresies, including the idea that Jesus wasn't fully divine. While such things are impossible to reconstruct with certainty, given the paucity of contemporary evidence, it's certainly possible to detect such influences in the way the Koran mistakes several key biblical doctrines and events.

First, the Koran, like the Hebrew Scriptures (Old Testament), emphasizes the oneness of God. Christians too believe in only one God, of course, but also believe God is a Trinity of Father, Son, and Holy Spirit. While we see hints of this in the Old Testament, it doesn't become more obvious until Jesus and the Holy Spirit appear distinctly in the New Testament. So, someone influenced primarily by Judaism—as many now think Muhammad may have been—would not understand the complexities of Trinitarian doctrine. It's not simply that the Koran gets the Trinity wrong—substituting Mary for the Holy Spirit—but that it doesn't understand the basic concept of three persons in one God at all.

DO WE ALL WORSHIP THE SAME GOD?

One thing is important before we go on—do Jews, Christians, and Muslims all worship the same God? *Allah*, the name for God in the Koran, is simply the Middle Eastern, Arabic name for God. Arab Christians pray to Allah; but when they do so, they're not praying to the God

A GOD DIVIDED

of Islam but to the God revealed in Scripture, the God of Christian faith. So, purely in terms of the name, the answer is yes. (There's an entire book on this subject by Beeson theologian Timothy George, for those who want to follow all this up in more detail.)

Theologically, though, it's surely more complex. God hears the prayers of all who call upon him, but he hears them in the name of his Son, Jesus Christ. Does a Muslim pray in this way? The answer is, surely and sadly, no—but neither do any who pray to God, or a god, or many gods, except through Jesus. It would be wrong to single out Muslims. Perhaps this should be a major incentive for evangelism. Many Muslims have been converted in all sorts of unlikely circumstances, and we know if they turn to God in true repentance, he hears them as he listens to all who seek him.

This is, naturally, not a politically correct thing to say. However, most Muslims believe the same thing the other way around—that Christians don't go to heaven, since they have rejected Muhammad as God's final revelation. So, in fact, Muslims probably aren't the ones who would be offended, since they're certain that they're right and that Christians, Jews, and followers of other religions are wrong. Christians and Jews, as monotheists, do have special status in Islamic countries; and in medieval times, for example, Muslim nations treated Jews far better than Christian states did. But Judeo-Christian "people of the Book" status doesn't mean Muslims think Jews and Christians can get to heaven without converting to Islam.

Such a view as mine actually offends the relativistic, all-religions-are-true-in-their-own-way philosophy found in the postreligious West. On many issues, especially moral ones, practicing Jews, Christians, and Muslims have common cause—as "co-belligerents"—and have more in common *in that sense* than they do with secular nonbelievers.

It's also clear from the Koran that the growing Mary worship in the church of that day caused Muhammad to exaggerate Mary's status to Christians.

Some Old Testament stories appear in a strange way— for example, Abraham comes near to sacrificing Hagar, from whom Arabs claim descent, rather than Isaac.

Modern writers (such as Feiler in *Abraham: A Journey to the Heart of Three Faiths*) are correct in saying that Judaism, Christianity, and Islam all revere Abraham. But that's also misleading, because the Abraham of Islam is subtly different from the Abraham Christians know from the book of Genesis and the rest of the Bible.

DIFFERENCES BETWEEN THE BIBLE AND THE KORAN

Abraham, to Christians, is the founder of the Jewish race and also an example of a faithful person going out into the unknown in complete trust in God. He is also very human, making mistakes—something that does not occur in the Koran. In terms of Christ's humanity, Abraham is also Jesus' ancestor, as Mary is descended from him.

To Muslims, though, he is one of the many prophets on the way to the final revelation and prophet, Muhammad himself—as are several other Old Testament characters, such as Moses and David. Even Jesus—*Isa* to the Koran—is given prophet status. Muslims do revere Abraham but give him an altogether different role than the one given him by Jews in the Old Testament and Christians in the New.

In the Koran, Jesus—*Isa*—is just another human prophet en route to *the* prophet, Muhammad. He is certainly not God and, according to Islamic teaching, didn't die on the cross and rise again. (Some Islamic groups believe he was buried in what is now Afghanistan, but not all Muslims believe that.)

Here we see a very important distinction between the Koran and the Bible. The Gospels are about Jesus, a narrative entirely around one person. The Koran is a law book, mainly spoken as from God. While Muhammad was the conduit for the book, it's certainly not about him.

This makes a critical difference. The Koran is a code—how to live. The New Testament does contain plenty of injunctions on how to live a godly life, but it's above all a biography—the story of a person, Jesus, who is God come down to earth in human form. One of the great themes of Romans is that Christians are, through Jesus, under grace, not law. Of course, we are not supposed to sin—as Paul duly emphasizes. But a grace relationship is inherently completely different from a legalistic, ritualistic form of obedience. As Christians, we know God through Jesus and the Holy Spirit dwelling within us. Islam, however, has no such concept of relationship or assurance of salvation.

(The mystic, or *Sufi*, version of Islam tries to get around this, but the harsher, more strictly legalistic versions of Islam therefore reject Sufism as theologically illegitimate. "Folk Islam," about which Christian specialist Bill Musk has written, also tries to get away from the dry formalism of official Islam. It's similar to the syncretistic forms of paganism and folk Catholicism seen in places such as Latin America.)

The importance of this distinction between Christianity and Islam cannot be overemphasized. Our faith revolves around a person, and our relationship with God is a personal one. We can truly know God. However devout and full of good works Muslims might be, they don't have the same assurance. In the Koran, God is inscrutable, and his ways unfathomable, to an extent that isn't true of the God who reveals himself in Scripture, above all through Jesus Christ.

Muslim unease at this legalism resulted in a form of Islam best known as *Sufism*.

Sufism is best described as a mystic Islam in which one can feel faith spiritually as well as know it intellectually. While Sufis would not claim to have the depth of relationship with Allah that Christians do with God through Christ, it's nonetheless the nearest that any version of Islam comes to spiritual intimacy. The works of distinguished moderate Muslims such as Akbar Ahmed contain much Sufi influence.

There's no Holy Spirit equivalent in Islam, but the ecstatic worship of many Sufi orders, such as the famous Whirling Dervishes in Turkey, is as close as Muslim worshippers come to Holy Spirit experiences in Christianity.[†] The Sufi movement also is the source of much lyrical poetry.

[†] I'm not making analogies here with any specific Christian groups.

A GOD DIVIDED

Many of the stricter interpretations of Islam renounce Sufism as being syncretistic. One can see why. Sufi holy men, or *pirs*, renouncing the world and living a life of separated holiness, aren't unlike some early Christian ascetics or mendicant Hindu or Buddhist priests in South Asia. *Pirs* can marry, and there are dynasties of holy men whose houses have been revered by the faithful down to present times. When hard-line Muslims, such as the Wahhabis of Saudi Arabia, take over, Sufi shrines are often among the first things destroyed.

(The Shiite version of Islam common in Iran and southern Iraq also has its Sufi equivalents, and Shiite Islam is more open to mysticism than the majority Sunni variant.)

One important thing to remember about Sufism is that usually close followers of Sufi rites are unlikely to believe in violence. (Sufi orders have, however, turned militant when their country was under attack, but that relates to the struggle against Western colonialism.) It's very important to remember post-9/11 that many Muslims loathe violence as much as we do. Brave Christians fighting persecution of fellow Christians in hard-line Muslim countries may take exception to this statement; but if one looks, for example, at the way the Muslim community has integrated in places such as the United States, the case still stands!

It's the Koranic revelation's impersonality that leads Muslims, correctly, to reject attempts to describe their religion as Mohammedanism. Muhammad is revered, but he is not God, and Islam rejects totally the very notion of a Trinity.

The notion of redemption through a person is at the heart of the gospel. It is *the* good news. Judaism also has the concept of sin, of being in rebellion against God even if one is born a Jew, plus a foretaste of redemption through the system of sacrifices.

Sin, however, is a concept completely absent from the Koran. There's no sense of a relationship with God, of sin breaking that bond, and of the necessity of a Savior to redeem sinful human beings. Access to heaven is through the balance of deeds, the kind of works-righteousness mentality for which Christ condemned the Pharisees and which the Reformers rejected in the sixteenth century. Sociologists writing about the Islamic world often talk about shame culture, with shame, especially of one's kinship group, being the ultimate trespass. But sometimes it's right to do wrong if it protects the tribe's dignity and prevents shame falling upon them. (This isn't peculiar to Islam—other Asian cultures often possess it as well, in slightly different forms.)

But sin and shame are not the same. The doctrines of repentance and forgiveness, so central to Christian faith, are simply absent, although there are plenty of rules for the most minute of human activities.

This is the basis of the *sharia* law Muslims believe is direct from God, which is at the heart of the Koran. (Man-made law, or *fiqh*, comes in a definite second to devout Muslims, and they see Muslim countries that introduce Western law codes, such as Egypt or Algeria, as betraying Islam's true path by putting human law above the divine.)

Westerners tend to dwell only on Koranic law's more gruesome aspects, such as cutting off hands for theft. But first, such barbaric practices were abolished only comparatively recently, especially in Europe. Second, such demands

A GOD DIVIDED

are only a minor part of a far larger corpus of law regulating all sorts of details, from how many times to worship to how to make financial transactions.

In many ways, *sharia* law is not unlike the equally detailed law codes of the Old Testament, where God's people were also a discrete political/cultural entity. Because Christ abolished the ceremonial law, we forget how much there was in Old Testament times regulating life in equal detail. Also, many of the Old Testament laws made plenty of dietary and medical sense for a nomadic people living in the desert. Many of those principles still hold good today as common sense, let alone as divine ordinances.

What is lacking from the Koran, therefore, is any sense of grace or of an indwelling Holy Spirit who can speak to the conscience and provide guidance in loving obedience and righteousness, in gratitude for all God has done for us. Without grace there is only law, and that is what the Koran provides.

So while Christians should protest at, for example, the lack of human rights in Muslim countries and the savage way in which people are treated in some of them, surely the spiritual response should come first. Muslims are people living very much under law, and what they really need is God's grace through Jesus Christ.

Christians should also remember our own temptations to be pharisaical. While we often remember in theory we are under grace and not law, we all too easily forget it in practice. We should always be aware of the parable of the speck and the plank when talking to people under the sway of legalism.

The five pillars of Islam, the core beliefs derived from the Koran, are also essentially legalistic. They are faith (*iman*), verbalized through a specific profession of faith (*shahadah*); the five daily prayer times (*salah*); almsgiving (*zakat*); fasting during the holy month of Ramadan (*sawm*); and pilgrimage to Mecca (*hajj*). All these are legally and permanently binding on all faithful Muslims. Obedience to them brings merit but no guarantee, in and of themselves, of paradise.

Some radical early Muslims also added a sixth, *jihad*, which has been variously interpreted in Islam. But those who add this today are only a very small minority, although one with consequences for all of us.

Reading the Koran isn't easy because of the way it's laid out—by size, not theme or narrative history. Nonetheless we should do it if we are to have dialogue with Muslims today. We cannot refuse to read the Koran if we are asking them to read the Bible!

If we do read the Koran, it will be clear that Koranic exegesis isn't easy. (One can read the accounts of former Muslims, such as Ibn Warraq, but his works aren't easy either! Remember, too, that a devout Muslim would regard such works as most Christians would radical, liberal theology that denies Christ's divinity.)

One problem with the Koran is that some *suras* seem to contradict each other. (Theological liberals say the Bible does, too, so we should be careful about how we raise this point with Muslims we might meet.) Moderate Muslims often quote the *sura* "there is no compulsion in religion." Extremists of the al-Qaeda variety similarly quote what's

A GOD DIVIDED

known as the "sword verse," which includes the injunction to "slay the unbelievers."

If one looks at Islamic history, these verses seem to have been interpreted by different groups in divergent ways—disagreement among devout Muslims isn't new. We now know that much of Egypt continued to be Christian for several centuries after the Islamic invasions of the seventh century. In Spain (al-Andalus) and the Balkans, the majority of the population always remained Christian—Catholic in Spain and Orthodox in the Balkans. Small Christian minorities still exist in the Middle East to this day, such as the Copts, Assyrians, and Chaldeans.

What Is *Jihad?*

But one of the most argued-over Islamic doctrines, *jihad*, is at the heart of how one interprets the Koran. *Jihad* literally means "struggle," but it can be interpreted either as a holy war (sometimes called the *lesser jihad*) or as a personal struggle for holiness (the *greater jihad*). This controversial Islamic concept remains a matter of dispute among Muslims to this day. This is very relevant in distinguishing between early Islam and early Christianity.

Ask most moderate Muslims today what they mean by *jihad*, and they will answer that it is the internal, personal struggle to be a better Muslim. It's the nearest they come to the Christian doctrine of sanctification.

Moderate Muslims don't usually believe in violent *jihad*. But if one reads the *fatwa*, or religious pronouncements, made by extremist groups, the notion of *jihad* as holy war remains as strong as it was to some early, violent Islamic sects.

Now is the time to mention two other vital sources of Muslim doctrine—the *hadith* and the *sunnah*.

It has been rightly said that Judaism, Christianity, and Islam are all book-oriented faiths. The Old Testament, the New Testament, the Koran—these are fundamental to what Jews, Christians, and Muslims believe, respectively. However, Protestant Christianity differs from the other two and from Orthodox and Catholic versions of the Christian faith.

In another chapter, we'll examine the key difference the Reformation made to Christianity and similar reform attempts within both Judaism and Islam. One Reformation tenet, *sola scriptura*—Scripture alone—is critical in distinguishing historic Protestant theology from Judaism and Islam.

PILING ON MORE LAW

While it's true Islam revolves around the teaching of the Koran, Muslims have two other sources of religious instruction and law. The first are the *hadith*—accounts of what Muhammad said, did, and approved—collected over decades and put together in various collections long after his death. The second is the *sunnah*, or life of Muhammad, again relying on oral tradition after the Koran was written.

In 680 the Islamic world split between the approximately 85 percent (in today's statistics) Sunni Muslims and the 15 percent Shiite minority. The dispute was essentially more political than religious. The Shiite minority insisted that the line of successors, or *caliphs*, to Muhammad could only come through his direct descendants (via the marriage of his daughter Fatima to his cousin Ali). The Sunni argued that anyone chosen by the Islamic community, or *umma*, could be a caliph.

Today the Sunni and the Shia have different collections of *hadith*, each group supporting its own position. Much of what one reads in al-Qaeda statements is based on *hadith* rather than on the Koran. Each *hadith* is supposed to have a line of provenance or authenticity, since only the Koran itself is guaranteed pure and infallible.

This, of course, presents a problem. Not only is there one "infallible" book, but a huge collection of sayings and tales of Muhammad's life to go alongside the Koran. Different Islamic teachers have interpreted the Koran in divergent ways. In Sunni Islam, for instance, there are four remaining law schools of interpretation.

Although the analogy isn't a direct one, this is not unlike the Jewish reliance on the vast Talmudic literature as well as on the Old Testament/Hebrew Scriptures. Similarly, one of the main issues at the Reformation was whether Scripture alone was sufficient or, as the Roman Catholic Church still argues, that the accumulated teaching of the church holds equal authority with the Word of God.

In other words, non-Protestant Christianity, Judaism, and Islam have enormous bodies of nonscriptural teachings that nonetheless have authority virtually equal to that of the sacred holy book.

This is why different Muslim groups can quote equally from the Koran and come to drastically different conclusions.

One controversial Koranic doctrine recognizes this dilemma. Many Muslims believe in *abrogation*—that some Koranic *suras* were abrogated by those that came later. Thus, a moderate Muslim can sincerely believe that the era of violent *jihad* is now firmly over. However, unfortunately, men such as Osama bin Laden argue it's very much with us, even though most Muslims would strongly disagree, for example, with his willingness to kill innocent people.

Here the indisputable parts of the *sunnah*, Muhammad's life, are very instructive and totally different from the lifestyle of Christ and the early church shown in the Scriptures.

Some Christians have chosen to regard Muhammad's multiplicity of wives—far more than the five the Koran sanctions—and the youth of one of them, Aisha, to assault his morals. This is offensive to Muslims, and for that reason alone it should be avoided. (Muslims will also point out that many of his wives were the widows of key Islamic leaders killed in battle, whom he married to protect.)

However, it is the parts of his life that Muslims agree upon that is the real difference between Muhammad and Jesus. Since Muslims agree that Muhammad was indeed a military leader who led raiding parties on the caravans or trade missions of his enemies, Christians are surely on firmer ground in contrasting Muhammad and Jesus.

CONVERSION VERSUS THE SWORD

Muhammad was, as mentioned earlier, a military, political, and spiritual leader all rolled into one. It's here, let alone in the issue of Christ's divinity, that he and Jesus Christ differ so strongly.

Jesus is the Prince of Peace. He renounced worldly ambition and forbade his disciples to take up arms in his defense. Muhammad, however, used military means to bring about his aims, and this included raids on the trading caravans of rivals. Politically correct apologists such as former nun Karen Armstrong have defended this part of Muhammad's life. But surely, these days, such military action in pursuit of spiritual goals is unjustifiable.

In terms of their own daily practice, many Muslims would, in fact, agree. Some parts of the world, including Indonesia, the largest Muslim country in the world, were converted to Islam through mission, not the sword. (Christians should remember that while some of the Islamic world became Muslim through conquest, much of it did not.) The *sura* that there's no compulsion in Islam rings true for many moderate Muslims across the world, including those in the United States, who are often a model of how immigrants can integrate successfully.

No one contests the military side of Muhammad's leadership. One other legacy he left to the Islamic world is the close joining of what we in the West call "church and state."

As we will see in the chapter on the Reformation, the West also used to have this model, which historically was called Christendom. However, Protestant Christians soon realized this simply was not the biblical model. One reason the New World was colonized—apart from making money—is that Christians wanted to flee to a place where they could worship God as they felt right.[†] Eventually, every state recognized its citizens' right to worship God according to their own conscience, and the United States now leads the world in freedom of religion.

But this was not the policy Muhammad established first in Medina and then, toward the end of his life, in Mecca. He was both spiritual leader and political leader in one—to use a medieval analogy, the pope and the Holy Roman Emperor combined.

It's fair to say that monotheists—Jews and Christians— were allowed freedom to practice their own faith in the new *dar al-Islam*, or house/abode/realm of Islam. They had special protected status but had to pay extra tax.

However, with the oft-quoted exception of *Umayyad*-ruled Spain in the Middle Ages, things didn't always work out well for the two minorities. We needn't go as far as Bat Ye'or, whose books on *dhimmitude* have become essential reading for Christians living in Muslim countries, but it was clearly not easy being a Christian or a Jew in a resolutely Muslim empire.

Jews, Christians now have to admit, did far better in medieval Islam than they did in European Christendom. For instance, while Armenian Christians were massacred as recently as the twentieth century, there never has been an Islamic equivalent of the Holocaust against Jews, nor is there in Islamic countries the degree of anti-Semitism that mars Europe even to this day.

[†] My book *Whose Side Is God On?* deals with this subject in greater depth.

A GOD DIVIDED

However, non-Muslims could not advance to higher levels of society, and evangelism of any kind was strictly forbidden—even in the otherwise tolerant and progressive Umayyad *caliphate* in Spain. This, as Bat Ye'or points out, created an inward-looking, almost servile attitude in the Christian population that led to the spiritual deterioration of the once-vibrant churches of North Africa and the Middle East.

Today there's no single pattern for the treatment of Jews, Christians, and other minorities in Islamic countries. Indonesia has seen phenomenal Christian growth. Jordan tolerates local Christians, but overt evangelism is forbidden, and foreign missionaries have to be careful of what they do. Saudi Arabia, whose Wahhabi form of Islam is spreading globally, is one of the most oppressive countries on earth and the spiritual home of extremists such as Osama bin Laden. Conversion to Christianity there still carries the death penalty, and since a few years after Muhammad's death, the Arabian Peninsula hasn't allowed the overt practice of any religion other than Islam. The large Jewish communities of the seventh century have long since vanished.

This lack of tolerance is a major mark against many of the predominantly Islamic societies in the world today. Christians in Egypt do not have the same level of human rights as Muslims in the United States. Mullahs can make religious statements in Western countries that no Christian leader would dare to make even in otherwise progressive Muslim states such as Jordan. Reciprocity of religious freedom simply doesn't exist.

The very grave problems Europe's growing Muslim population faces stem from the origins of its faith as a religion of political and military power. While we needn't share the pessimism about Europe's future painted by Bat Ye'or and others, this is nonetheless a major concern to non-Muslims as well. The issue of Muslims in Europe is high on the agenda for European military and political leaders. In essence, since the Islamic conquests of the seventh century, Muslims have not been used to living in countries in which they are a minority and don't control the country politically.

DOES A FAITH NEED A COUNTRY?

In Spain Muslims were a minority, but they also ruled for nearly eight hundred years. Likewise, while most Slavs in the Balkans didn't convert, except the Bosnian Muslims, the Ottomans ruled the Balkan Peninsula for more than five centuries. During the period of Western rule in South Asia and the Middle East, Muslims were under Western domination; but in Egypt, Iraq, and present-day Pakistan they had freedom of religion and constituted the majority of the population at the same time.

Now, in Western Europe, the large Muslim population is neither in charge nor a majority. In the past, as Bernard Lewis reminds us in his books, even the idea of diplomatic missions that would have meant Muslim diplomats could live temporarily in Christian countries was for a long time unthinkable. Today's London, Paris, and Hamburg have large Muslim populations.

For Christians, living in similar circumstances has never been such a problem. Christianity spent its first centuries as

A GOD DIVIDED

a viciously persecuted, illegal, underground faith. Christians had no power, nor any expectation of any. Christians, in other words, don't need political or military power. If Christians today live in an unsympathetic country, they know that has been the fate of countless fellow Christians since the beginning.

Christianity and Judaism have never depended on outward circumstances to survive; but that has not, until the twenty-first century, been true of Islam.

For intelligent, moderate Muslim leaders such as Akbar Ahmed (who lives in the United States), this is certainly a challenge but not an insuperable problem. Such Islamic thinkers are inspired by nonviolent leaders of the late nineteenth and early twentieth centuries, often from what is now Pakistan. They tried to work out how to be a good Muslim and examine objectively what made the West great.

If they are the Islamic future, we can probably all sleep safer. We should never forget that such decent Muslims exist, since the media stereotypes of Islam are often profoundly unhelpful. The nice, friendly Muslim we encounter at work or who owns the local store or who campaigns for decent moral values at the neighborhood school—all these are perfectly legitimate representatives of their faith.

To some modern Koranic exegetes, Muhammad allowed for a third option: the realm of truce, or *dar al-sulkh*. According to experts, Britain was accorded truce status by leading Islamic legal scholars because of its relaxed immigration policy that allowed many Saudi dissidents to live there freely. However, it was withdrawn by some hard-line Muslim leaders in 2004, quite possibly because of the British troops fighting against Sunni Muslim rebels in Iraq. It could be that the withdrawal of truce status led to the atrocities committed in London on July 7, 2005. (There's also in Islamic tradition a special category of realm of covenant in which a Christian ruler under the suzerainty of a Muslim is allowed peaceful privileges. No states like that currently exist, however, although they did in the past.)

Other Muslims prefer the idea of a realm of peace, or *dar al-salaam* (also the name of the Tanzanian capital). In such a setting, everybody could get on peacefully with everybody else. However, some Muslims, such as in Canada, are asking for essentially a reverse-*dhimmi* status. This would be a special legal position under Canadian law whereby present-day Canadian Muslims would be able to live under *sharia*, Islamic law, not under Canadian law, especially if the two law codes conflicted. Needless to say, the Canadian government hasn't looked favorably upon their wishes.

Western countries differ in what they allow Muslims to do. In Britain, since the current government is strongly favorable to Christian schools—even giving money to set up state-funded, Christian-based schools—they have extended this right to Muslims as well. So now there are state-funded Muslim schools, and Muslim girls have full freedom to wear specifically Islamic clothing. In France, by contrast, strict secularism has been in force ever since the zealously anti-Catholic regimes of the French Revolution. Muslim girls have been forbidden to wear even the *hijab*, or Islamic head scarf, let alone the full *chador*. This has created much tension between the Islamic community and the very secular majority around them. France and the Netherlands have also had the idea of asking for *imams* to be trained in the countries in which they will serve, which avoids the British problem of many of the mosque leaders coming from overseas with little or no knowledge of Western life.

However, to other Muslims, friendliness and accommodation to the West are unacceptable, since to them it contradicts Islam's origin as a religion of power. Here is where the terrorists come in. For them, the answer to all the problems is restored Islamic rule and the kind of Muslim theocracy witnessed in Taliban Afghanistan. To Islamic extremists, the idea that any Muslim should have to live in a non-Muslim country is completely intolerable.

According to some Koranic interpretations, once a land goes into the *dar al-Islam* it stays there forever. Spain is in that category, despite the fact that the last Moorish ruler was expelled more than five hundred years ago. It's thought that the Madrid bombers, who murdered so many commuters in 2003, had this mind-set. For some pious Muslims, Spain remains al-Andalus and always will.

In other words, the way in which Muhammad began the faith now causes significant problems for it in our radically different twenty-first century. Muslims in non-Islamic countries now have to face an awkward choice—to adapt to new circumstances or take the path of violence.

Christians, too, dislike much of the secular West. Much in Western culture is antireligious or simply and often very invidiously materialistic. But for Christians, living in such times isn't new, for the early church lived in the equally unsympathetic, materialistic, and hedonistic society of the Roman Empire.

Christian faith, therefore, isn't threatened by adverse circumstances. Persecution has been the lot of the Christian from the outset—just read the New Testament! Secularism and modernity may be new or may also be new forms of very old spiritual enemies. We don't have to adapt the Christian faith to counter the moral and theological problems of the twenty-first century.

But then, biblical Christianity is not a religion of secular power. Christendom was surely an aberration, not the norm. If we consider the phenomenal growth of the church in China, where millions of people have become Christians in the face of frequent and often vicious persecution by an openly antireligious government, we can see how Christianity can thrive against all odds in modern times.

This built-in advantage for the Christian faith has been there since its beginning. It is another reason why Christianity is evidently the one true faith.

There's not space to go into detail here on many other parts of the Koran.

One of these is the role of women, which is always controversial. Moderate Muslim writers point out that the requirement to be hidden from head to foot is in fact a cultural command, specific to certain ethnic groups, since all the Koran commands is that women be modestly dressed. Women in Iran, for example, don't have to cover up the way Saudi women do; and in countries such as Jordan women can often dress as they do in the West.

While all this is true, women certainly do remain second-class citizens in places such as the mosque, where they cannot worship alongside the men. We don't see the same treatment of women in the Koran that is evident in the New Testament—there's no Islamic equivalent of Martha and Mary, Priscilla, or Dorcas.

SUNNI VERSUS SHIITE

It's important to remember that Islam's Shia and Sunni divisions are based essentially on political, rather than spiritual, grounds. Significantly, the issue was decided by the Battle of Karbala (in what is now Iraq), which the Shiites lost.

Although the Wahhabi sect of Islam denies that Shiites are Muslims, most Sunni and Shia recognize each other as fellow believers. The late Ayatollah Khomeini of Iran, a major Shiite leader, was often careful to refer simply to Muslims rather than to Sunni and Shiite. However, some differences have arisen over the years.

The main difference between the sects is that Shiites still believe in *ijtihad*, or the possibility of individual interpretation. Because of this, Shiite legal experts (there are theoretically no clergy in Islam) gradually became significantly more important than their Sunni counterparts. While Shiites would deny they have anything like Christian clergy, their leading Islamic jurisprudence experts, the ayatollahs, are in practice similar to Catholic cardinals, with the most eminent of them being as near to a pope as the Muslim world gets.

But we should remember that only about 15 percent of Muslims worldwide are Shiite, and we hear about them disproportionately because of their preponderance in Iran and Iraq. More than 85 percent of Muslims would reject the very notion of an ayatollah. In Sunni Islam, no one individual has that kind of doctrinal influence. (With cable and satellite stations such as Al Jazeera, there are now, however, a growing number of Sunni Muslim equivalents of American televangelists.)

THE EXPANSION OF ISLAM

Over time, the four schools of Islamic thought developed. The Hanbali variant, while in theory limited to Saudi Arabia, is now increasingly widespread thanks to that kingdom's vast financial resources. The future of Saudi Arabia, and the direction in which it will go, is one that concerns governments and oil companies around the world. It ought also to be a major item of prayer for Christians, since the Saudis often fund the mosques in areas where the church is also growing. Both West and East Africa have dynamically growing churches with many souls being saved, but also many people turning from animism to Islam and becoming more antagonistic to the gospel than ever before.

After the first four Muslim caliphs (only one of whom died peacefully), powerful dynasties assumed power in the new Islamic world. The first of these was the Umayyads, whose capital was in Damascus; the second and longer lasting, were the Abbasids, close kinsmen of Muhammad, who are known in the West primarily through the caliph immortalized in the tales of *1,001 Arabian Nights*.

Having begun in the Arabian Peninsula, Islam spread like wildfire, from the borders of Iran in the east to Spain's

A GOD DIVIDED

Atlantic coast in the west. But for the Battle of Tours in 732, the whole of Western Europe would have fallen to the Islamic invading armies.

All this is very relevant to one of the main bones of contention between Christians and Muslims—the Crusades.

Unfortunately, the Crusades, and whether they were the right thing to do, have become part of the highly political "culture wars" in today's United States. This is regrettable, since a politically neutral and Bible-based assessment of them is urgently necessary, as Muslim apologists are always mentioning them in the dialogues that take place between Christians and Muslims. On the other hand, especially since 9/11 and the war in Iraq, we have seen books with titles such as *The Politically Incorrect Guide to Islam (and the Crusades)*, which look at Islam and the Crusades through a particular set of deeply held political beliefs.

As we saw earlier, Jesus made clear that his was a spiritual and not a political kingdom. That is not to say the gospel doesn't have a profound effect on politics. But Jesus came as a Savior, not as the kind of military and political leader that Muhammad was.

Consequently, the gospel spread entirely through conversion growth, through what Christians would say was the power of the Holy Spirit enabling followers of Christ to proclaim the good news of salvation, despite the most terrible persecution. As Paul says, all Christians are soldiers, but their weapons are spiritual, not physical!

This, however, wasn't the case with the equally rapid geographical spread of early Islam, although places such as Egypt took a long time to convert from Christianity.

Nonetheless, the early caliphs ruled one of the biggest empires of military conquest ever seen, from Spain to Iran.

What we call the Holy Land was under the rule of the Christian Byzantine Empire until AD 638 when it became one of the first areas to fall under the rule of the new Islamic armies only six years after Muhammad's death. As mentioned earlier, once a territory goes from the *dar al-harb* to the *dar al-Islam*, in the eyes of most Muslims it remains in the realm of Islam forever.

In Palestine, while many local Arabs did convert, large numbers did not. In fact, a huge Palestinian Christian population existed until our own time. (A survey after 9/11 showed that 73 percent of Arab Americans are of *Christian* ancestry and nominal belief, many from families that recently fled from Palestine to the United States to avoid persecution.) Similarly, a substantial Jewish population remained in the area as well. Although the region was under Islamic rule, by no means were all the people living there converted to Islam.

FROM SALADIN
TO BIN LADEN

✡ ✝ ☪

B y the tenth century, the Byzantines, the successors in the East to the old Roman Empire, were getting worried about Islamic incursions into their territory. Foolishly, in retrospect, they asked for the cooperation of Christians living in Western Europe. The Byzantines were Orthodox, the Westerners Catholic (the two churches split in theory in 1054, but in practice much earlier).

The pope saw this as a wonderful opportunity to reassert his authority. He was able, in effect, to hijack a Byzantine appeal for help. When Pope Urban proclaimed the Crusade, with the famous phrase *"Deo lo veult!"* or "God wills it," he launched a series of invasions of Palestine that have caused problems ever since.

THE CRUSADES AND THEIR LEGACY

One key motivation for the French and some other knights who went off to the Holy Land was forgiveness for their sins, since they earned merit for going. Also, the phrase "Holy Land" itself shows that they too regarded the geographical territory as especially holy. Jerusalem is the one city in the world special to Jews, Christians, and Muslims alike. But do we find this concept of sacred territory in the New Testament?[†]

So, before the armies had ever been launched, the Crusades began with three unbiblical propositions. First, going to war and killing innocent civilians—which even the Christian chroniclers record—is hardly likely to win anyone a place in heaven! In any case, salvation comes through grace, not works—which was the whole point Luther made when he began the Reformation. Second, God's people on earth are the church. There's no sacred national soil. This is a wholly Islamic concept and does not belong to the Christian faith. Third, the whole idea of a holy war is entirely unbiblical, as Jesus forbade his disciples to fight physically in his cause. Christian weapons are spiritual—words, not swords!

In fact, one could say the crusaders were using Islamic methods. We can interpret the Crusades as a Christian *jihad*; and since that concept is Koranic, not biblical, we can hardly

---

[†] I'm here excluding the much wider issue of the place of the Jewish people in God's plans. That wasn't an issue to the crusaders, who often massacred Jews as well as Muslims, so we will ignore it here.

A GOD DIVIDED

defend the theological basis of the crusaders' actions, let alone the many atrocities they committed.

Nowadays in Muslim-Christian dialogues Christians are asked to apologize for the Crusades. Surely the Christian response should be to denounce them passionately as a wholly misguided action based on bad theology, which totally contradicts the teaching of the Bible.

Osama bin Laden calls Westerners crusaders, claiming that everything they do is an attack on the sacred heart of Islam, the *dar al-Islam*. Yet eminent Jewish historian Bernard Lewis is surely right when he says the Islamic world ignored the Crusades for centuries.

There are two reasons for this. First, the Muslims won the Crusades! The crusader possession of Jerusalem lasted less than a century, although the West held territory for another hundred years in Acre.

Second, until the late seventeenth century, the Muslim world regarded itself as more powerful than the West. In fact, the heartland of Islam didn't come under Western attack until 1798, when the French briefly captured Egypt, and the core of the Muslim world didn't fall under European rule until 1918 when the once-mighty Islamic Ottoman Empire fell. So, until the twentieth century, Muslims could bask in the reflected glory of Saladin, the Muslim leader who regained Jerusalem for the *dar al-Islam*, defeated the "infidels," and restored Muslim pride.

This is why the Islamic world's anger against the Crusades is wholly recent and as much political as spiritual. The Muslim world resents the dominance of the West, and attacking Christians for an invasion that took place more than nine hundred years ago is part and parcel of today's Islamic rage.

There's always the temptation of saying things like, "Well, if you dislike the Crusades, what about the Islamic invasion of Spain three hundred years earlier and the invasion of the Balkans over two hundred years after the crusaders left?" Historically, that would be right!

However, this isn't the spiritually correct way to approach the issue. Historically, Protestants weren't always guiltless—remember that the great Swiss Reformer Huldrych Zwingli died sword in hand in a war between Protestant and Catholic cantons. Also, Christianity spreads through the power of the Holy Spirit, not through a sword or scimitar. Brave Christians through the centuries have lost their own lives in evangelism, rather than taking those of others in battle. The blood of the martyrs, not that of vanquished foes, is the seed of the church!

Christians, therefore, are not dependent on geography, and never have been. This is a major Christian-Islamic difference. Look where the church is growing fastest—in the two-thirds world, often where there were hardly any Christians at all at the beginning of the twentieth century.

Historians often call the nineteenth century the "Great Century" of Christian mission; and that's historically correct in terms of bold Christians leaving the comfort of their homes to evangelize in often hostile, unhealthy, and deeply uncomfortable terrain. But the gigantic growth of the church has taken place in the past hundred years, often, interestingly, long after the Western missionaries have gone, but in the very areas in which they were most active. The brave men and women of the Great Century may not have seen the fruit themselves, but it's now emphatically there for the entire world to see.

This is all a stark contrast to the sword-wielding crusaders. In the end, in the Fourth Crusade in 1204, the greed of the crusaders and their merchant allies destroyed the Byzantine Empire—the one great military bulwark that was preventing a successful Islamic invasion of Europe from the southeast. While the empire was briefly restored, in 1453 the Muslim Ottoman Turks conquered it and by 1529 had nearly captured Vienna in the heart of central Europe. The Ottoman Empire ruled over Christian peoples in Europe until its twentieth-century defeat. The Crusades' final result, therefore, was the successful Islamic invasion of the Balkans and nearly five hundred years of Muslim rule over Christian Slavic peoples—not quite, perhaps, the legacy the crusaders would have wished.

DOMINANCE SHIFTS
FROM ISLAM TO THE WEST

We should remember that, in the time of the Crusades, the Islamic world was far ahead of the West in terms of medicine, technology, learning, and civilized living in general. Many secular Western historians now feel medieval Islam enabled us to have the Renaissance, the flowering of humanist scholarship and art that took place in southern Europe and that preceded the Reformation in northern Europe by about a century. Some crusaders' more uncouth European cousins saw them as having gone soft because they had begun to adapt to the more advanced ways of the Muslims around them.

Mathematics in the Muslim world was far ahead of anything European. The word *algebra*, for example, is of Arabic origin. The ancient Greeks knew all about geometry. Their knowledge was translated early on into Arabic, and the Arabs enhanced it considerably by devising algebra. In medicine, Western Europeans would translate Arabic texts into Latin and bring the Islamic world's medical advances into Europe.

Many Arabic thinkers became famous in the West by this means. Europeans adapted Arabic names: Ibn Sina became Avicenna and Ibn-Rushd Averroës. In due time, Muslim sages became well-known names in Western universities and monasteries. Historians know that the fall of Constantinople, the Byzantine capital, to the Ottomans in 1453 brought Greek learning to the West, as many learned men fled to the still-Christian parts of Europe. But in fact, Greek knowledge had already been coming to the West for centuries via the Arabs.

However, by the fifteenth and sixteenth centuries, the time of the main Renaissance in southern Europe and the Reformation in the north, the Europeans had begun to catch up rapidly. By the end of the seventeenth century—the failure of the Ottomans to capture Vienna in 1683 and their first major losses to the West in 1699—Europe was gaining the advantage for the first time in more than a thousand years.

To be fair to the Muslim world, it was not only the *dar al-Islam* that was losing out to the West, by now as much

A God Divided

Protestant as Catholic.[†] Then, by the sixteenth and seventeenth centuries, the West caught up.

Unfortunately, as Bernard Lewis reminds us in his book on what went wrong for Islam, the Ottoman Turks had no real wish to explore and benefit from Western learning—except, perhaps, military technology, especially after their forces were beaten by European armies. Likewise, the Chinese were fascinated by Western inventions such as clocks, often brought by Jesuit missionaries sent to evangelize China, but the great Qing dynasty emperors spurned all further Western knowledge, saying the Middle Kingdom—the Chinese name for their own country—had no need of such things from inferior peoples.

Because of 9/11 and the great interest now taken in Islam in the West, we have tended to concentrate on the relative decline of the Islamic world and other nations like China in the face of a Christian Europe.

Secular historians, by definition, always come up with secular answers for the drastic changes witnessed in the past. This is hardly surprising! However, if we have a Christian view of history, we can see God's hand in things that secular historians attribute to ordinary causes.[††]

[†] One of the most significant works of scholarship is the multivolume history of science in China. Having just written how far in advance the Islamic world was of the West, the same could be said of the then still-separate Chinese Empire. Just as in the Muslim *caliphate*, the Chinese had all kinds of technologies, including such things as paper money, printing, advanced industrial foundries, gunpowder, and superior medical techniques, all completely unknown in the West for centuries.

[††] I deal with this subject at length in my book on the Reformation, *Five Leading Reformers*.

For example, is it coincidental that print came to the West just before the Reformation began? The ability to print pamphlets that ordinary people could read was of pivotal help to the early Reformers in getting their doctrines known among ordinary folk. Likewise, the fact that the Bible, translated into the language of the common people, could be printed and sold in massive numbers greatly aided *sola scriptura* in a way that would have been impossible when each Bible had to be created literally by hand.

In addition, why didn't Holy Roman Emperor Charles V swat the early Protestants like a fly, as was the fate of earlier Reformer Jan Hus, martyred in 1415? One answer secular historians now propose is that he was perpetually worried about a possible Islamic invasion. The Ottomans vanquished the Hungarian army at the Battle of Mohacs in 1526 and very nearly took Charles' Austrian capital, Vienna, three years later. Charles also ruled much of Italy and all of Spain, and Islamic fleets constantly threatened his hegemony in the Mediterranean. But for the permanent distraction of Ottoman armies, Charles might have tried to destroy Protestantism at its birth.

Secular theories, therefore, are not incompatible with Christians seeing God's hand at work. This is also true of how Europe suddenly and rapidly overtook both the great Ottoman Empire close to home and the even bigger Chinese Empire far to the east.

Europe had many advantages. One was internal competition. Whereas the Ottoman and Chinese Empires were huge organizations controlled from their imperial capitals, Europe was a vast jigsaw of comparatively small

A God Divided

states, competing actively with their neighbors in all spheres of life.

There were downsides to this of course, the most notable being that they were often at war with each other. But, in a sense, this helped too. No one power became too powerful, as the Protestants discovered to their benefit. The European states also increased their weapons technology, an advantage when the slow reconquest of the Balkans from the Ottomans began in the late seventeenth century.

The desire to compete led in time to the discovery of the New World. And while there is no condoning the atrocities committed by many settlers against those millions who already lived there, as J. H. Elliott points out, even meeting people of such different races gave Europeans a whole new perspective that was lacking in the increasingly inward-looking and moribund Ottoman and Chinese Empires. The Chinese had stopped long-distance sailing some centuries earlier (before that, their junks had gone as far as Africa and maybe even Latin America); and the Ottomans, too, felt that they had all that was necessary.

But above all, the West now had something incomparable.[†] Nothing innate in Europe enabled it to suddenly forge ahead. Some advances could be attributed to luck—the fact that there were many different European countries, as opposed to one all-encompassing empire as in China or the

---

[†] Up until then, Europe was in many ways a backwater. Parts of Africa, such as Benin, were producing artworks, for example, that were different from the European, but that were, surely, the artistic equal of anything seen in the Renaissance. Yet Europe suddenly forged ahead.

FROM SALADIN TO BIN LADEN

Ottoman *caliphate*. But it was the revitalization of Christianity, the coming of the Reformation that made all the critical difference.[†]

But, having issued the necessary caveat, I do think the old Weber-Tawney thesis[††] is as good a general explanation of the rise of Western Europe as any. This secular theory attributes the West's success to what evangelicals would call Bible-based Protestantism. In essence, the Weber-Tawney thesis marries the rise of capitalism with the strong, Scripture-based Protestant and Reformed faith of its early founders.

Needless to say, not everyone agrees with this view, and the Italian Renaissance invention of banking certainly helped subsequent developments. But business, industry, trade, and great international mercantile empires took off in the northern Protestant states, such as Britain and the Netherlands, and territories in northern Germany, such as Prussia. Italy had wonderful art and the Medici banking system—but none of the many little states on the Italian peninsula came anywhere near, say, the Netherlands, although the Dutch lived in a region almost as small politically as Tuscany and lacked the natural resources usually deemed necessary for an economy to grow. Someone once said the natural resource of the Netherlands has always been the Dutch people—and, at this

---

[†] Some will realize at this point that we are arguably dressing up a very old theory in new clothes. And I will concede that nothing I'm suggesting is infallible—but for that matter, I believe that no man-made theories can explain everything.

[††] Invented by the German founder of sociology, Max Weber, and British thinker Richard Tawney.

A GOD DIVIDED

time, most of them were of the new and dynamic Reformed Protestant faith.

The Ottoman and Chinese Empires had vast natural riches. But even today, that doesn't make the real difference. The Middle East has fabulous oil wealth, but the average GDP (gross domestic product) per person in that part of the globe is much less than that of a comparatively small European state like Belgium. A nation can have all the resources in the world, but if its citizens' mind-set is wrong, it does it no good!

So, although it might be unfashionable to say so, Protestantism made all the difference. Plenty of non-Christians realize this. For example, one of my teachers when I was an Oxford undergraduate was distinguished Marxist historian Christopher Hill. When I visited his study, I was pleasantly astonished by the large number of Puritan reprints he owned from evangelical publisher Banner of Truth. Hill, although Marxist, believed strongly that their *Christian* worldview made the Puritans so economically effective. In other words, Hill realized that core spiritual beliefs determine economic actions, not the other way around.

Not all of North America was settled by godly Puritans—people from Free Church backgrounds were even persecuted in several early colonies—but large parts of the New World *were* inhabited by those who deeply held to the Puritan conviction that work was worthy in God's eyes. This isn't to say that the faith behind such an attitude continued effortlessly from generation to generation; the fact that the Great Awakening was spiritually necessary shows that, from a spiritual point of view, things had already gone sadly astray.[†]

Nonetheless, it's probably fair to say that the Puritan work ethic of Weber-Tawney survived, even if its biblical origins were forgotten by growing numbers of people.

Also critical was the rise of science in the West, particularly in Protestant Great Britain. Christian writers such as Oxford academic Alister McGrath and Cambridge scientist Denis Alexander have written much on the subject, but secular historians also have come up with similar perspectives. The late Roy Porter showed how Puritans in late seventeenth-century Britain were actively involved in the scientific revolution of the time.[††] In a recent book, Gertrude Himmelfarb argued that the British Enlightenment and subsequent infant American republic were innately different from their continental European equivalents, such as the often anti-Christian version in France.

In the United States, Himmelfarb's work is controversial, since she is a leading neoconservative thinker, but she is in fact saying much the same as Porter, who was

---

[†] One only has to read Cotton Mather's book *The Great Works of Christ in America* to see that subsequent generations observed the outward forms but were increasingly losing the profound personal faith of the early settlers. We can, as Mark Noll reminds us, overdo the continuing evangelical faith of Colonial America.

[††] Sir Isaac Newton had some strange theological ideas, but one of the key founders of the Royal Society, John Wilkins, sadly less well known, was a devout Puritan Christian (and brother-in-law of the famous political leader Oliver Cromwell). Robert Boyle, one of that great century's most eminent and written-about scientists, was a keen Christian, as concerned with the evangelism of the Muslim world as he was about his better-known scientific discoveries.

A GOD DIVIDED

profoundly admired by many British writers and thinkers on the political left. There's a cross-party consensus that the Protestant-friendly, seventeenth-century scientific revolution in Britain is innately different from the frequently Deist, anti-Catholic, eighteenth-century equivalent in Europe.

A strongly Protestant self-identity, a scientific revolution, a vast increase in trade, colonies in North America—all these made Britain radically different from the countries around it.

This is the intellectual ancestry of the world's most powerful nation, the United States of America. Mark Noll and other historians have done well to point out that it's possible to exaggerate the Christian roots of the United States. Many of the founding fathers were Deists, and only one can be said to have been evangelical in the theological sense. However, while many no longer had the faith, many of the tenets of their more Christian ancestry remained. Hard work, scientific inquiry, and a sense of optimism all helped craft the early American republic. While these are also secular attributes, the Puritan ancestry is still there to see.

THE RISE OF TOLERANCE

One of the most influential political and legal thinkers who inspired the early American leaders was the late seventeenth-century British writer John Locke, particularly his *Letter Concerning Toleration*, published in 1689. While Locke was not an evangelical, he did understand the key truth that conversion is a matter of *inward* change. Outward adherence is meaningless if the person within is unchanged—as we would put it, unless the individual is truly born again.

This meant, to Locke and others, that compulsion in religion is also meaningless. People can be forced to attend church, but that doesn't change their *inward* belief. This is obvious to us now, but it was a new realization then.

Not long after 9/11, I turned a chapter I wrote on John Locke into a background briefing for British prime minister Tony Blair. It might seem odd to write something on a seventeenth-century philosopher at such a critical time in history as the attack on the Pentagon and the World Trade Center. Yet what Locke thought and wrote and the influence he exerted, especially on the early United States, is pivotal in understanding the vast gulf between the tolerance and pluralism in the West and the complete absence of tolerance and pluralism in many Islamic regimes.

Sadly, the freedom to be a Baptist, Congregationalist, Presbyterian, or whatever, rather than being conformed to the Church of England, led in due time to the freedom not to be anything at all. This is why some see secularism and the Enlightenment as the grandchildren of the Reformation.

Once a society starts to have diversity, tolerance of some kind is bound to emerge, as it did in Britain in the 1680s (Parliament's Act of Toleration was passed at the same time that Locke's famous epistle was written).

However, the kind of Enlightenment that produced the United States is very different from the violently antireligious, class-ridden revolution that took place in

A GOD DIVIDED

France a few years later. France had the Reign of Terror, the guillotine, large-scale massacres, the Cult of the Supreme Being, revolutionary dictatorship, and a series of upheavals that ended with an all-powerful emperor, Napoleon Bonaparte. It's true that the United States experienced a bloody civil war in its first century, but if one looks at the continuing upheavals of French history and the fact that today France is still profoundly secular, there's quite a difference between the two countries.

African-born, American-based historian Lamin Sanneh, in his book *Piety and Power*, shows that the kind of tolerance Locke discussed was essentially Christian in origin. It derives from the scriptural account of conversion, based not on place of birth but on inward change. This was one of the great rediscoveries of the Reformation—*sola fidei*, faith alone. Locke even said he would give Muslims freedom of worship, since state compulsion could not force them to change their minds. This was dramatically unlike, say, the Spanish Inquisition, in which people were tortured and killed in the name of the church because they would not renounce their Jewish, Muslim, or (later on) Protestant beliefs.

This rediscovery of the vital importance of personal faith shows an understanding of the Holy Spirit's work in conversion.[†]

This is unlike some of the Islamic world today, where a person can get killed even for being the wrong kind of

---

[†] On this Christian theological point we must be careful! However, most Protestants would agree that it is God who brings about genuine conversion rather than death threats or imprisonment.

Muslim. In Pakistan, hard-line Sunni Muslims have attacked not just churches, but also Shiite Muslim mosques, with both Christians and Shiites numbering among the victims.

(Here it's vital to add that in India, both Muslims and Christians have been murdered, sometimes by the thousands, by extremist Hindu mobs. Muslims are by no means always the perpetrators, and many innocent Muslims have died as well as Westerners in bombings in places such as Bali.)

In the past, Christians also have been guilty of all kinds of violence. In Oxford, I lived near the place where Protestant martyrs Thomas Cranmer, Nicholas Ridley, and Hugh Latimer were burned to death in the sixteenth century. But in Cambridge, I daily pass a Roman Catholic Church built to commemorate Catholics similarly put to death in Elizabethan England.

What we have thankfully lost, though, unlike Islam, is not just a sense of compulsion, but also what Sanneh calls *territoriality*. We no longer automatically associate place and adherence to faith. While many Americans mourn the loss of predominance that Christianity once had in the United States, no one would ever think of trying to make it compulsory. Only one part of Europe—Greece—continued the old trend into the twentieth century and insisted that its citizens follow a particular religious belief. Nowadays, Christians in the West evangelize and recognize that active believers are now in the minority.

In the Islamic world, people are born Muslim, except in countries such as Jordan or Syria where significant Christian

A GOD DIVIDED

minorities remain. Conversion out of Islam is forbidden, and Islam as the official religion is often rigidly enforced, especially in places such as Saudi Arabia.

Christendom has long since gone, but the *dar al-Islam* still remains. The legacy of the prophet Muhammad continues.

THE REFORMATION AND CHRISTIAN TRUTH

✡ ✝ ☾

Before we look at the differences between Judaism, Christianity, and Islam in the twenty-first century, we need some key history lessons. One of the most important lessons concerns the major change made to the Christian faith by the seventeenth-century events we call the Reformation. Christian truth has played a major part in history as well as in Scripture.

We'll look at this issue in relation to Judaism later, so here we'll consider Islam and how the Reformation contributed so much to the cause of Christian faith, especially in relation to the other two monotheistic religions.

DOES ISLAM NEED A REFORMATION?

Recently there was discussion in the London *Times* about Islam's need for a reformation of the kind the Christian West underwent in the sixteenth century. This was argued with much feeling by famous novelist Salman Rushdie. Rushdie has particular reason to have strong emotions on this subject, since he was the subject of a death threat in the 1980s made by the then spiritual leader of Iran, Ayatollah Khomeini, in a now notorious religious utterance, or *fatwa*. (It should be said here that most *fatwa* are harmless—about whether good Muslims can play chess, watch movies, and other such topics.) Khomeini condemned Rushdie to death for writing the novel *The Satanic Verses*, which, among other things, made fun of the prophet Muhammad in a way that many Muslims around the world considered blasphemous.

As many human-rights groups and missionary societies can attest, blasphemy is *still* punishable by death in some Muslim countries. This was true in Afghanistan under the Taliban and remains the case in Saudi Arabia and, in some extreme cases, even in a country such as Pakistan, where Christians have found themselves in trouble for supposed blasphemy against Muhammad in recent years.[†]

To Westerners, all this was barbaric. In many quarters, Islam has received very bad press for its extremism, only magnified since the bombings of 9/11, in the United States, and 7/7, in London.

[†] We do well to emphasize "even," as not every devout Pakistani Muslim would agree with such rulings.

A GOD DIVIDED

However, the revulsion at the *fatwa* and the fact that so many Western Muslims clearly agreed with it played strongly into the hands of liberal humanists, who used Islamic extremism as the excuse to attack religion in general, Christianity included. To them, the fact that one of the world's most senior religious leaders was advocating death for blasphemy condemned *all* religion as primitive and barbaric. All the witch trials in Europe and the United States from Salem onward were brought back into a public debate about the place of religion in modern times.

Moderate Muslims were horrified at the way a group of extremists seemed able to hijack the Islamic faith so quickly and discredit it in Western eyes. (As we mentioned, the presence of so many millions of Muslims in the West who don't live under Islamic *sharia* law has become one of the major issues facing Islam today.)

However, such leaders remained devout Muslims of a peace-loving kind. But, as both Islamic and secular commentators realized, what Rushdie and others of his views are calling for is a theologically liberal kind of Islam. This would, as both moderate/devout and extremist/devout Muslims realize, be a watered-down Islam, more secular than religious, and not unlike the similar kind of wishy-washy, liberal Christianity that has so failed in the West in the past century or so.

Here we need to be careful. A good friend in Christian ministry once suggested to me that the extremists are surely the *real* Muslims, since they take their Koran seriously. However, while that is true about their devotion to Islamic sacred texts, many leading nonviolent, moderate Muslims also take the Koran equally seriously and have very different views. As Akbar Ahmed, the leading U.S.-based Islamic thinker, writes, all true Muslims believe the Koran—the real question is how they interpret it. This isn't surprising, since the Koran has many exegetical problems. But we shouldn't think there are only extremist and liberal Muslims, as this isn't the case—plenty of Koran-believing Muslims don't wish to blow up anyone or execute people for rejecting Islam. Nevertheless, the point made by Rushdie and others that there's still much to be desired in the Islamic world is surely valid.

CONTRASTING EARLY HISTORY OF CHRISTIANITY AND ISLAM

The fact that many Christians as well as secular leaders were horrified when a U.S. Christian commentator called for a dictator's assassination shows that most Christians would now emphatically reject the excesses of the past. However strongly we might disagree with people who denigrate Scripture, no one is calling for such people to be burned at the stake!

We owe this to two things: the original teaching and practice of the early Christian church and the rediscovery of these foundational truths by Christians in the seventeenth and eighteenth centuries following the Reformation.

First, we need to look at the Christian past, at our origins and the reformation of our faith, then consider whether the answer to Islam's dilemmas is for the Muslim faith to have a

A GOD DIVIDED

similar period of reform. This is presuming (which we really can't do) that Islam *has not had a reformation, of sorts, already.*

Great academic writers such as Bernard Lewis make clear that there's an all-important difference between the origins of Christianity and Islam. It's a vital spiritual difference with major political results.

Christianity, Lewis and others show, began as a small, persecuted faith, whose early adherents were frequently martyred and which was illegal in its early centuries.

It's worth noting that Judaism began similarly (most writers contrast only Christianity and Islam). From Abraham to the beginnings of the exodus, Jews, while not initially persecuted, were certainly not followers of the state religion. There was no Jewish state as such until the conquest of the Promised Land was well under way and the twelve tribes of Israel settled in their new territory. Then came the period of the judges and the kingdoms of Israel and Judah; after that, the Jews went back to being under alien political and religious rule until the foundation of the state of Israel in 1948. We'll look at the importance of this later, but now we must return to the major difference between the two universal faiths: Christianity and Islam.

In contrast, Islam began as a religion of secular power. Muhammad was at the same time a spiritual leader and a political and military chieftain. While he and his followers were initially persecuted—Muslims date their calendar from his flight to Medina in AD 622—Muhammad solved the problem not just by winning converts but by being a warrior as well. Soon his armies were victorious, and he ended his days as the ruler of the new Islamic state established by both the sword and conversion. Following his death, his disciples began one of the most successful military campaigns in history, conquering a vast Islamic empire that within decades stretched from the Atlantic coast of present-day Spain in the west to the borders of the Indus River in what is now India in the east.

While Christians spent their first three centuries being persecuted and martyred, Islam spent its first three hundred years becoming one of the most powerful military empires the world has ever seen, with Islam firmly in place as the religion of the new territories, the *caliphate*.

The importance of this in terms of how Christianity on the one hand and Islam on the other hand face the vicissitudes of twenty-first-century life cannot be exaggerated.

God does not need a sympathetic state to spread the good news of salvation in Christ. Christianity, even in the twentieth and twenty-first centuries, has often spread fastest in areas that previously were completely inimical to the gospel, such as the People's Republic of China or semi-Islamic Nigeria and Indonesia. Islam, on the other hand, because of mass migration in the past decades, now has a brand-new problem—that of millions of Muslims living in non-Islamic countries. For Muslims used to living in Islamic regimes, this is a wholly new phenomenon, but Jews and Christians have experienced it for centuries.

Unfortunately, in the fourth century the church formed what in retrospect was a Faustian pact with the state with the accession to power of the Roman emperor Constantine. (Strictly speaking, Constantine made Christianity the *officially tolerated* faith of the empire—it didn't become the sole, *official* faith until later. But the effect was the same.)

The good news is that Christians were no longer being persecuted, and that must have come as a huge relief! But Christians also handed the running of the church over to the state—the emperor, rather than the Bible, became the arbiter of Christian doctrine, as the story of the following centuries shows.

The other problem was that Christianity became associated with *place*. If a person was born or lived in an area with a Christian king or emperor, that individual was part of the church. This, of course, flatly contradicts the Bible, which stated clearly in the Old Testament that being Jewish did not save anyone. Later in the New Testament Jesus told Nicodemus that even the most righteous of Pharisees had to be born again personally to enter the kingdom of God.

We therefore see the dawn of Christendom, a concept unknown to Scripture but very similar to the Islamic concept of the *dar al-Islam*, or abode/realm of Islamic rule. Today, people born, say, in Saudi Arabia, are deemed to be Muslims and may not convert out of the Islamic faith on penalty of death. For centuries a similar concept applied in the West— if a person was born, for example, in medieval France or Byzantine-ruled Syria, that individual was deemed to be a Christian.

Christendom's first major split was in 1054, when the Catholic Church in the West split from the Orthodox Church under Byzantine rule in the East. Unfortunately for the Eastern Orthodox, since the emperor controlled the patriarch in Constantinople (the capital of the empire), church and state became interdependent.

So, when successive Islamic invasions took over most of the Orthodox world except for Russia, the church was greatly weakened. The once-vibrant church of the Middle East became a mere sad shadow of its once-great past. Churches dating from New Testament times withered on the vine.

In the West, it was slightly more complicated. The Roman Empire fell in the fifth century, a thousand years before its counterpart in the East. The one remaining major figure from Roman times was the pope, the bishop of Rome. Therefore, when Charlemagne reconstituted a primarily Germanic Holy Roman Empire in AD 800, the emperor didn't have authority over the pope—but since the popes were also secular rulers of much of middle Italy, weak popes always had to be wary of strong emperors. Who had the most authority was never fully resolved, despite the successes of many of the stronger popes of the Middle Ages.

Either way, Western Europe was still Christendom, with church and state inexorably intertwined, including lands not under the emperor such as England, France, and Scandinavia. Whether a person was born a peasant in England or a merchant in France, he or she was a Catholic.

This had terrible repercussions for both evangelism and knowledge. In this era, Europeans didn't spread the gospel beyond their own borders, and the *dar al-Islam* was scientifically, technically, medically, and militarily more powerful than Christian Europe, to the detriment of Western civilization and the Christian faith itself.

Medieval Christians did evangelize to the boundaries of what is now Europe, with present-day Lithuania and the

A GOD DIVIDED

Baltic states being the last to receive the gospel. But here we notice two things:

First, evangelizers always tried to convert the king or ruler first; then the people followed. Some kings and also, one prays, many ordinary people were converted—but, as the survival of many pre-Christian pagan practices shows, some supposed conversions may well have been only skin deep.

Second, no attempt was made to convert non-Europeans. Since Christianity began in the Middle East and came to Europe through conversion, this shows a major failure of theological understanding. We see this in the tale of William of Rubruk, a brave Flemish monk who managed to travel as far as the court of the great khan in present-day Mongolia during the Middle Ages. While some of the khan's relatives converted to Islam, the Mongol ruler himself was open to other religious perspectives and asked William to request the pope to send missionaries. Sadly, the request was refused, and a great opportunity lost. Real, in-depth evangelization of East Asia didn't get under way for hundreds of years, in the nineteenth century and later.

The plight of Christians in the Muslim world deteriorated over time. Umayyad-ruled Spain showed a large amount of tolerance to Christians and Jews; but this was increasingly not the case in other Islamic territories, especially among the remnants of the Christian churches in the Middle East, the descendants of the original Christians. We now know that countries such as Egypt took a long time to convert fully to Islam, especially since authorities got more money if the population remained Christian, because non-Muslims had to pay a special tax for *not* being Muslim! In the Balkan region—areas such as present-day Greece, Serbia, Romania, and Bulgaria—the bulk of the inhabitants remained Christian; but this wasn't the case in the Middle East, where most people ended up converting to Islam. As a result, Christians, who were given *dhimmi* or "people of the Book" status by the Koran, found themselves beleaguered.

THE DEMISE OF CHRISTENDOM

Although Protestants took a while to get going overseas after the Reformation, the great events of the sixteenth century did have one dramatic effect on the Christian faith: As time progressed, Christianity ceased to be seen as the religion of a place. Christendom, in the old sense of the word, disappeared. This happened for three reasons:

First, Western Christendom split into two, with some parts of Europe remaining Catholic, but many others becoming Protestant. It took a long while for the Catholic powers of Europe to accept this and led to nearly two centuries of carnage, culminating in the especially bloody Thirty Years War in what is now Germany. But when it ended in 1648, all the different kingdoms, dukedoms, and principalities (and occasional republics, such as Switzerland) recognized that some countries would now be Protestant for good. This was called the principle of *cuius region, eius religio* ("whose rule, his religion"), since the ruler determined what the state religion would be. While religion and place were

A GOD DIVIDED

still linked, at least the old concept of Christendom had vanished—no one, as time went by, was deemed a Christian simply because of where he or she was born. Furthermore, the Catholic Church now had competition; and one of the effects of this was to persuade many Catholics to start preaching outside of Europe, with Francis Xavier, for example, taking the message to India and East Asia—the start of cross-cultural mission.

Second, in the seventeenth century Protestant Christians began to realize the wider implications of the truth Luther had rediscovered at the Reformation—the "just shall live by faith," or *sola fidei*.

If what saved people was not where they were born but their becoming Christians in their own individual right before God, then the whole concept of a state-imposed faith was theologically untenable. (Many of the mistakes of Luther, Calvin, Zwingli, and other magisterial Reformers were made because this truth had not yet dawned upon them.)

The main effect of this change was the understanding that religious toleration was vital. As John Locke and other thinkers realized, conversion is an *inward change*. People can be forced to assent to something nominally on the outside, but inwardly they can still be entirely unchanged. In Britain this led directly to the Edict of Toleration in 1689, which meant that non-Anglican, Nonconformist Christians had full civil liberties for the first time—Christians such as John Bunyan would no longer find themselves in jail. The eighteenth century saw great historical movements such as the Methodist revival, an event that would have been legally impossible before.

Third and finally, Protestant Christians woke up to their global responsibilities to fulfill the biblical mandate and take the gospel to all nations. The nineteenth century isn't referred to as the heroic age of Christian mission for nothing. Never before had so many brave Christians ventured overseas to take the message of salvation cross-culturally to millions who had never heard it before. The Christian faith was becoming what it was always meant to be—a truly universal faith.

The famous nineteenth-century French writer Alexis de Tocqueville observed that it was the lack of a state-imposed version of Christianity that made the Christian faith so vibrant in the United States. We forget how different the American and French Revolutions of the eighteenth century were, despite being just a few years apart. The American Revolution brought lasting democracy and genuine freedom, to the benefit of not just Americans but of countless others, especially in the twentieth century. The French Revolution soon devoured its moderates, led to a brutal dictatorship and mass killing, then to Emperor Napoleon, war, and military defeat.

Many would now argue that a strong line of succession can be drawn from the Enlightenment to the violent nationalist movements of the nineteenth century and to Fascism and Communism in the twentieth. (State atheism— in the form of the revolutionary Cult of the Supreme Being—began in eighteenth-century France, long predating Lenin, Stalin, and Mao, though one can easily draw an ideological line between the French revolutionaries and twentieth-century Marxists.) Perhaps, people are realizing,

A GOD DIVIDED

the European Enlightenment wasn't entirely such a good thing after all.[†]

As soon as people had the freedom to believe in their own interpretation of the Christian faith—not just Protestant or Catholic, but the many varieties of Protestantism we know today—they eventually came to exercise their freedom not to believe in any kind of Christianity at all. That is why the Enlightenment has been called the Reformation's illegitimate child, for with the freedom of belief that inevitably arose when Protestants understood what conversion meant came the freedom to reject Christian faith altogether. Today Western Europe is one of the least religious places—and certainly one of the least Christian places—on earth.

One interesting note: There are many more practicing Anglicans in Nigeria than there are in the home country, England. In addition, most Nigerian Anglicans are evangelical, which may be true of grassroots members in Britain but certainly not of the hierarchy.

[†] Other historians, by no means Christian, are now writing that the British Enlightenment was quite different, and did not, of necessity, have the strongly antireligious element of its continental counterpart. One could argue that it also started earlier, back in the seventeenth century with John Locke and also the founding of the Royal Society in the 1660s, the world's first truly major scientific body. The Royal Society's founding members included Christians, such as the great scientist Robert Boyle, who cared as much about evangelism as he did about the latest scientific discoveries. It is this British, religion-friendly Enlightenment that was the one inherited by the infant United States, which is why the history of America has been so very different. Much of what happened was directly linked to Protestantism, and thus the British Enlightenment can be said to be an indirect product of the Reformation, in a way that the violently antireligious Enlightenment and subsequent French Revolution were not, with its vicious persecution of the Catholic Church.

America, by contrast, has remained deeply religious. Evangelicals in the United States understandably bemoan the fact that there are far fewer American Christians than one would like. But in proportion to the total population, there are considerably more Christians in the United States than in the United Kingdom, let alone in other parts of Europe. But by and large, even nominal allegiance is on its way out in Western Europe and—as a senior aide to Billy Graham once reminded me—in much of North America as well.

From a spiritual point of view, this rejection of Christian truth is distressing and a constant impetus to evangelism. However, at least Christians in the West still have the freedom to share their faith, unlike many others throughout history—including those in many parts of the world today, especially in the Muslim world. We owe this freedom to the Reformation and can be thankful when we look at the hundreds of millions of people who live in repressive regimes.[†]

We also have freedom of thought to work through key issues without interference and to form Christian responses to whatever the modern world, with all its changes, throws at us. The late Francis Schaeffer reminded us that Christian truth—what he called *true truth*—is permanent and unchanging. But as the genius of his work, L'Abri, also showed, Christians need to learn the language of the world

---

[†] Not that persecution is any problem for God, as we will see: A key Muslim and Judeo-Christian difference is that Jews and Christians have never needed sympathetic regimes to flourish, as the growth of the church in China reminds us.

A GOD DIVIDED

they're evangelizing. There's no point in going as a missionary, say, to France, if we don't know a word of French. Likewise, we need to communicate God's unchanging truth in a language our contemporaries can understand.

THE VITAL IMPORTANCE OF *SOLA SCRIPTURA*

Sola scriptura, or Scripture alone—the fact that Scripture must be in a language ordinary people understand—is also a key difference made by the Reformation.

Today we Western Christians take the plethora of helpful Bible translations for granted. Yet it is in fact one of the great fruits of the Reformation, a value for which great sixteenth-century Reformers such as William Tyndale were prepared to die as martyrs.

Scripture, the early Protestants realized, is doubly authoritative—it's God's recorded Word; and, through the Holy Spirit working in our lives, it speaks directly to us. We don't need the mediation of a vast priesthood to come between us and God's message found in the Bible.

While the proliferation of denominations, and their differing interpretation of issues such as baptism or church leadership, shows there's a downside to Protestantism, nonetheless the difference *sola scriptura* makes cannot be underestimated.

We see this in relation to Judaism as far back as Jesus' own time. Furthermore, since many now think that Talmudic Judaism had a huge influence on formative Islam, what we see in the New Testament can, in a sense, be seen as equally applicable to Islam in our own times.

Scripture, the Reformers rediscovered, is entirely sufficient. We don't need an enormous *magisterium* of the accumulated teaching of the church to parallel and have equal authority with the Bible itself. (It's important to remember that the Reformers were *rediscovering* scriptural truth—Luther, *et al.*, didn't invent it!)

The Jewish and Islamic worlds are quite different, with crucial results.

JEWISH ATTEMPTS AT REFORM

The extra legalism that dominated Jewish thought is clear from the many encounters we see in the Gospels between Jesus and the Pharisees. We tend inevitably to concentrate on their rejection of him as the Messiah, and that is correct. But it's also theologically important to remember the oppressive legalism and the powerful sense of self-righteousness that come through adding vast layers of extra regulations to God's law. We are saved by grace, not by the law, although (as Paul shows in Romans) the law is our schoolmaster to bring us to God. The very fact that we cannot keep the law shows that it is by grace alone expressed in Jesus Christ that we can be saved at all.

How did the Pharisees get so far off in the first place? They were in many ways far less theologically astray than the Sadducees, who, like some theologians in our own day, had begun to pick and mix what they believed in. The Pharisees, by contrast, were very proud of their defense of truth. They taught that the Jews had gone into exile because of the people's rejection of God's law and that belief in that law was central to the very survival of God's people, the Jewish race. So what had gone wrong by the time Jesus came?

The answer is that for them Scripture wasn't enough— loads of man-made laws and regulations, down to the tiniest degree, were needed for people to implement God's law. The message of God's grace had been lost in the legal minutiae, with tragic effects. The Pharisees may well have begun with pure intentions, but by Christ's time they had become lost in a sea of legalism and a faith not of grace but of works.

Tragically, the situation only became worse over time. Not long after the time of Christ, they added yet another huge corpus of teaching to the Bible: the *Talmud*, a combination of legal commands and commentary. One had to believe not only the Hebrew Scriptures but also endless commentary accumulated by different rabbis over the centuries and compiled up until the third century AD. The actual, liberating Word of God—what we call the Old Testament—had been drowned in a sea of man-made rules, because the Pharisees felt that what God had commanded was either not enough or unclear without elaborate explanation. As time went by, therefore, it was not what Scripture said, but what Rabbi X said about what Rabbi Y had said on what Rabbi Z had commented.

All this had the effect, as we see from the New Testament, of creating a group of people very self-satisfied in their own righteousness and, worse still, blind to the real Messiah in their own midst, Jesus himself.

Early Jewish attempts at change and adaptation proved sadly short lived. In the eighth century, a group known as the Karaites tried to get rid of the endless Talmudic accretions and return to the truth of the Scriptures, known to Jews as the *Tanakh* and to Christians as the Hebrew Old Testament. This was very similar to what Luther and Calvin did at the Reformation—jettison centuries of accumulated man-made tradition and go back to the Bible—except that the Karaites remained a tiny minority. The traditional forces were simply too powerful to overcome, and so nothing really changed.

Another movement for change was the rise of mystic Judaism, called *Kabbalah*, best known in our time for trendy adherents such as rock singer Madonna. This grew up in the Middle Ages, especially in Spain, which in those days had a large and very influential Jewish population.[†]

Mainstream Jewish thought was rationalistic, based on reason. But in southern France, an unusual Gnostic cult had begun to permeate Western thinking—the Cathar heresy. (Followers of *The Da Vinci Code* and other Gnostic variants tend to be great enthusiasts for Cathar history and their gar-bled reinterpretation of both history and Scripture.)

Catharism was itself a variant of the ancient Zoroastrian religion, which goes back to Bible times and was the official religion of Persia (now Iran) in the days before the Islamic

---

[†] The Jews were expelled in 1492 after the Christian reconquest, on the orders of Catholic monarchs Ferdinand and Isabella. They fled to eastern Europe: They spoke Ladino, a Hispanic-Jewish dialect (as Yiddish is a Germanic-Slavic-Jewish dialect), and survived until the Holocaust in the 1940s. Thessaloniki, where Paul preached in Bible times, had a large Jewish population right up to the 1940s.

A GOD DIVIDED

conquests of the seventh century. There were two powerful and virtually equal gods, one good and one evil—the system thus became known as dualism. The Kabbalah, which was eventually written down in a book called the *Zoar*, developed over time; and much importance was given to a female being, the *shekinah*, analogous to the Gnostic notion of *sophia*, or wisdom—again a concept familiar to Dan Brown fans. One could say that Kabbalism, with its mysterious codes and symbols, was a mishmash of Gnosticism, Zoroastrian dualism, and a precursor to much of the New Age thinking that afflicts the world today. It certainly is not biblical.

From time to time, various Jewish eccentrics claimed to be the Messiah, and this too had an unsettling effect on mainstream Judaism, notably the attempt of Sabbatai Zebi. Once more, no lasting reformation took place.

By the nineteenth century, many Jews had realized that much had gone wrong.[†] Unfortunately, instead of returning to Scripture itself—in which they might have come to an understanding that the Messiah had already come in the person of Jesus—they, like many of the professing Christians around them, went in the exact opposite directions: theological liberalism on the one hand and mysticism on the other.

Judaism had its own equivalent of the European Enlightenment. One decision many Jews had to face was how much they should integrate culturally with the dominant

[†] As we know from studies of the Holocaust, by far one of the largest groupings of pre-Nazi-era Jews lived in what is now Poland, Lithuania, and Ukraine, an area that was, until the eighteenth century, all part of one powerful Polish kingdom.

Western culture in which they lived. This was especially true of the large Jewish minority in Germany, the heartland of much Romantic and Enlightenment thought. Many Jews wanted to blend into society and be more like the people around them.

In some countries, Jews converted to Christianity—as did the family of Britain's only ethnic Jewish prime minister, Benjamin Disraeli. (He was already a major politician by the time practicing Jews, like the British Rothschilds, were granted the right to enter mainstream politics.) However, most Jews wanted to retain their faith, but do so in a way that didn't alienate the Gentile majority around them.

As a result, *Reform Judaism* was born. Like the Protestant theological liberalism that arose in Germany around the same time, this was a theologically watered-down version of Judaism. It was, in one sense, a reformation; and some writers such as Norman Cantor have described it is as such—but it wasn't one in the sense that Luther or Calvin would have recognized. While Judaism was certainly reformed, it wasn't in a biblically orientated direction.

The other major change came not in prosperous Germany, but in the much poorer *shtetls* of Jews living in the Russian Empire, in what is now Poland, Lithuania, Moldova, Belarus, Ukraine, and parts of Russia. Anyone who has seen the movie *Fiddler on the Roof* will know what this was like—a backwater, often rural, existence, in much poverty, and with frequent persecution from the anti-Semitic authorities. (Until Hitler and the 1930s, persecution of the Jews was far worse in the Russian Empire than in Germany.)

A God Divided

This movement, in favor of a more experiential, less cerebral form of Judaism, is called *Hasidism*.

In the United States, Hasidic Jews are well known as the men who wear special hats and have long side curls. Hasidic life in North America has been wonderfully portrayed in the novels of Chaim Potok, including *The Chosen*. The Lubavitch Jews in the United States are Hasidic, as were (before the Holocaust) millions of Jews of central and eastern Europe, many of whom were murdered by the Nazis. However, commentators such as Norman Cantor have pointed out that many ordinary Hasidic Jews lived in dire poverty and often ignorance as well.

Hasidic Judaism was an attempt to get away from what many felt was the sterile intellectualism of Orthodox Jewish life. Jews in central Europe had, until the seventeenth century, often been prosperous, since they frequently enjoyed good relations with the nobility, not a few of whom were Protestants until the devoutly Catholic kings of Poland began to crush religious dissent. A pogrom against the Jewish middle class shocked the Jewish community, but the real disaster was the abolition of the enormous Polish kingdom by the greedy neighboring states of Russia, Austria, and Prussia. Most of the area inhabited by the Jews was allocated to Russia in the eighteenth century.

This was bad news. The Orthodox Church treated the new Jewish subjects much more harshly; and some of the czars, notably the last one, Nicholas II, were very anti-Semitic. Jews were allocated to live in an area known as the Pale of Settlement. Anti-Semitism grew worse, and in the long run, the lucky Jews were those who, like some in *Fiddler on the Roof*, found persecution so hard that they fled to the United States (and some to Britain). Not only were they free in America, but their descendants escaped the Holocaust that wiped out millions of Yiddish-speaking Jews and destroyed one of the greatest cultures Europe has ever seen.

Hasidic Jews were very dynastic. From their founder onward, successive generations of leading rabbis, whose dominance became marked, were deemed to inherit special powers and were regarded with mystical awe by their followers. Some of the Hasidic Jews who ended up in the United States were led by the Schneerson family of Rebbes. The last of the line was regarded as a possible Messiah by some of his more ardent devotees until his death in 1994.

Hasidic Jews, as *The Chosen* demonstrates, tend strongly to reject the outside world and replicate the isolation of the *shtetl* wherever they are, even in the freedom of the West. Interestingly, many also reject the existence of the Israeli nation, since they do not believe it can be a lawful state until the Messiah returns. (But that hasn't prevented many of them from living there.)

In conclusion, none of the Jewish reformation groups has made the same impact that Luther, Calvin, and others did in Christian history. Many Jews have made outstanding contributions to Western civilization, knowledge, and discovery—Albert Einstein is a classic example—but one could argue that the genius has been individual rather than as a corporate religious entity, in the way Protestantism affected Christianity.

A GOD DIVIDED

ISLAMIC ATTEMPTS AT REFORMATION

Islam, theologically liberal Muslims say today, has not had a reformation at all. *New York Times* journalist Judith Miller made this point in a book in which she interviewed pro-reform Islamic leaders, notably Abdul-Karim Soroush, whom some have described, perhaps optimistically, as an Iranian Martin Luther.

Former Iranian president Seyyed Khatami has spoken out on many occasions, especially since 9/11, arguing against a "clash of civilizations" between Islam and Christianity and for a peaceful "dialogue of cultures" instead. However, while Khatami and Soroush are deeply devout, they both come from the Shia minority—Shiites probably compose only 15 percent of Muslims worldwide.

More explicit calls for change within Islam have come from a very brave Canadian Muslim broadcaster, Irshad Manji, who took some risks to write the book *The Trouble with Islam*. However, Manji is also a leading gay-rights activist in Canada, and mainstream Muslims are not likely to listen to someone with whose lifestyle choices they profoundly disagree.

Akbar Ahmed is perhaps one of the few Sunni Muslims who has credibility because of his own devout beliefs but also strongly advocates peace. He is the Ibn Khaldun Professor at American University in Washington DC; author of *Islam under Siege;* and collaborator with Judea Pearl, father of murdered Jewish journalist Daniel Pearl, in active Muslim-Jewish reconciliation.

However, all this presupposes that Islam has *not* had a reformation, and that view is mistaken.

Of the countless books published after 9/11, one that stood out from the others was *The Age of Sacred Terror* by two former National Security Council officers, Daniel Benjamin and Steven Simon. One thing that distinguishes it is its writers' powerful sense of history, without which one cannot really understand what is going on in today's world. Their chapter on fourteenth-century Islamic thinker Ibn Taymiyya and his followers, down to al-Qaeda in the twenty-first century, is especially important.

We saw elsewhere that Islam, for much of the medieval period, was far in advance of the West in terms of civilization, learning, hygiene, science, medicine, and technology. But all this great Islamic advance came to a halt with the Mongol conquest of what is now Iran and much of Iraq in 1258, when the fabled city of Baghdad was captured and destroyed. There's a case for saying the Islamic world never fully recovered, although the eventual successor to the Islamic Empire, the Ottomans, remained militarily superior to Western Europe until at least 1683.

However, another good case could be made for the great issue of comparative Islamic decline—an issue that is dealt with in depth in Bernard Lewis's works, notably the post-9/11 book *What Went Wrong?* This is first of all a spiritual issue.

In the eleventh and twelfth centuries, before the fall of Baghdad in 1258, the consensus of the Sunni Muslim theological elite, the *ulema*, was that the gates of individual interpretation, or *ijtihad*, were now "closed." No new interpretation could now be made. (Shiite Islam is different.) This stultified further thinking, including the need to work out the relationship between new discoveries in medicine,

A GOD DIVIDED

science, technology, and so forth with what the Koran taught. Nothing new could now be said.

To an extent, evangelicals can understand what they were saying—once the original truth is delivered, there's no subsequent truth to add. However, the actual effect was to put an end to all new learning, innovation, science, and discovery.

Contrast this with the works of British writers such as Christopher Hill, Denis Alexander, and Roy Porter (of these, only Alexander is a Christian, which makes the claim even more significant). They have demonstrated that a great deal of modern science has come from Protestants who believe that because God created the world, investigating it is not merely lawful but something in which Christians ought to be actively engaged. (Alexander's book *Rebuilding the Matrix* is especially helpful for those wanting to follow up this subject in more detail.)

Thus the closing of individual interpretation by the Sunni Muslims is the equivalent of the Catholic Church announcing in 1100 that all truth was known and that nothing more could be said.

In terms of scientific progress there existed an ironic position—the West was beginning to catch up with the Islamic world because intelligent priests were reading about the Islamic world's scientific and medical discoveries and translating them into Latin.

On one hand, Islamic authorities were discouraging such innovation—because many of the leading Muslim scientists and philosophers were deemed to be too loose in their Islamic theology. On the other hand, the same Muslim discoveries were making major headway in the West. Twelfth-century

Europeans were beginning to understand that proper science, being the discovery of God's creation, was therefore entirely legitimate. (This is a key theme we'll return to later.)

Ibn Taymiyya, however, didn't believe that the gates of *ijtihad* were shut. This might seem an arcane theological point to us, but his beliefs, as Benjamin and Simon have shown, led directly to 9/11 and today's Sunni Islamic terror.

One of Ibn Taymiyya's main doctrinal points was that there could theoretically be Muslim rulers who were not real Muslims in the light of clear Koranic teaching. Evangelicals can understand this general concept—we believe, for example, there are nominal Christians whose outward profession and actual lifestyle are greatly at variance. However, unfortunately for us today, Ibn Taymiyya didn't leave it there.

Like many devout Muslims, he was worried about the Mongol conquest of the Abbasid *caliphate's* heartland. Theoretically, the Mongol rulers—the Il-Khans—were converted to Islam. In reality, they retained many of the shaman beliefs and practices of their ancestors. Their Islam, we might say, was skin deep. In contrast, the Mamluks, rulers of what is now Egypt, were still fully and loyally Sunni Muslims.

According to Muhammad, Muslim powers shouldn't go to war with each other. However, the Mamluks wanted to recapture land lost to the Mongol invaders—who, being now theoretically Muslim, could not therefore be attacked.

Ibn Taymiyya solved the problem. He did what wasn't supposed to be done since the tenth century and used his own individual interpretation, or *ijtihad*, to find an ingenious way around the problem. He said that rulers who were theoretically Muslim but in practice not really Islamic could legitimately be overthrown, since they were, in many ways, even worse than infidels who didn't pretend to be good Muslims at all. The Mamluks therefore could attack the Mongols legitimately and remain in accordance with the Koran.

Ibn Taymiyya didn't create a whole school of Islamic legal opinion to continue his thought. But four centuries later, in what is now Saudi Arabia (then just a collection of sheikdoms in loose affiliation with the Ottoman Empire) came the founder of just such a school.

This man was called Al-Wahhab, the eighteenth-century originator of Wahhabi Islam. He is arguably the real Luther equivalent of Islam—not some nice, pro-democracy, American-friendly Shiite theologian, as many in the West today would like to see. Realistically Islam has had its reformation already—it occurred almost three centuries ago—and it was not at all the change we in the West would have wanted.

Al-Wahhab lived for most of the 1700s. As he looked at how Islam had developed in the Arabian Peninsula, he found much that he disliked. Syncretism had increased greatly; and the reverence for sacred places had, he felt, become excessive. Sufi saints were given the credence that should only go to the word of the prophet Muhammad, the Koran. All this was losing track of the purity of original Islam and, therefore, had to go.

So far, much of this feels familiar. Like Luther, Al-Wahhab needed political backing—not in this case to protect him, as Frederick the Wise guarded Luther from the

Holy Roman Empire—but to introduce the reforms, and in a very muscular way. Al-Wahhab found the necessary sponsors in the al-Saud clan, and the reforms began.

Here the reforming movements begin to differ. Frederick the Wise didn't try to conquer Germany in the name of Protestantism and overthrow the emperor. The new faith spread, as in biblical times, by conversion growth—not so with Al-Wahhab's austere, stripped-down version of Islam. Proselytism and the sword went hand in hand, as Saudi soldiers and Wahhabi missionaries set out on a campaign of conquest, just as did the early Islamic caliphs they admired so much. The Saudi-Wahhabi coalition was able briefly to seize Mecca, the holiest of all Islamic places; and many ancient shrines were demolished as idolatrous. It took several decades for the Ottoman armies to restore much of the Arabian Peninsula to imperial rule—and the interior, where the al-Saud clan had its base, was only nominally reconquered.

At the beginning of the twentieth century, Abdul al-Aziz Al Saud, known as Ibn Saud, came to the leadership of his clan and began a series of military conquests that would make his family the most powerful and by far the wealthiest in the Muslim world. Two things enabled him to accomplish this. The first was the Ikhwan warriors, Wahhabi shock troops completely dedicated to the cause of Islam. The second was the discovery of the largest oil deposits in the world, found after Ibn Saud had united most of the peninsula under his rule.

The key conquest was in 1924, when Ibn Saud conquered the Hijaz, the sacred heartland of Islam, the land of Mecca and Medina. Until then it had been notionally under

A God Divided

Ottoman rule, but in practice under the authority of the Hashemite clan, direct family relations of Muhammad, whose family rules Jordan to this day. The seizure of the two holy places gave Ibn Saud and the Wahhabi version of Islam the legitimacy they wanted. With the *hajj*, or pilgrimage to Mecca, compulsory for all devout Muslims, and modern transport making that journey much easier, millions of Muslims from all over the world now visit Mecca and imbibe the Wahhabi interpretation of Islam.[†]

Wahhabi Islam, with its violent hatred of the West and insistence that it alone is the true form of Islam, is the official doctrine of Saudi Arabia to this day. With limitless revenue at its beck and call, it's swiftly becoming the predominant form of Islam in other parts of the world as well, since the Saudi government subsidizes new mosques and pays for the *imams* who teach in them. We know from many human-rights reports that Saudi Arabia is one of the most repressive countries on earth. (Excellent reports on civil liberties and religious freedoms, published each year by the U.S. State Department, are available free online.)

Yet all this is because what is now Saudi Arabia *did* experience a reformation back in the eighteenth century, when Al-Wahhab discovered the teachings of Ibn Taymiyya of

---

[†] I've written more about this subject in other books, and several secular books have also been published on the issue, especially on how Saudi petro dollars fund the extremist Wahhabi interpretation globally. Historian Bernard Lewis once controversially said it's as if the Ku Klux Klan was the official ideology of the United States and the billions of dollars earned by the U.S. oil companies was given to the American government to spread KKK doctrine across the world.

four centuries earlier. It's not, therefore, that Islam has failed to have a reformation, but that it has had one that, from our point of view, has gone tragically in the wrong direction. Fifteen of the nineteen 9/11 hijackers were Saudis, and all nineteen were followers of Wahhabi Islam, as is Osama bin Laden.

We see the effects of this in Egypt, which has a very large (at least nominally) Christian minority, the Copts, many of whom, thanks to generations of American Presbyterian missionaries, are now evangelicals.

In the late nineteenth and early twentieth centuries, Egypt, while theoretically still part of the Ottoman Empire, was really ruled by the British, as the power behind the scenes for the corrupt ruling family.[†]

After Islamic dominance began to decline, Egypt was conquered by the French, for just a few years, under Napoleon in 1798. In many ways this made more of a cultural impact on Europe than the other way around—one of the artifacts discovered in this period was the Rosetta stone, now in the British Museum, which enabled Western scholars to decipher ancient hieroglyphs for the first time.

Egypt was among those parts of the Ottoman Empire that saw a flourishing of intellectual thought in the late

---

[†] As we saw elsewhere, up until the late seventeenth century, the Muslim super-power, the Ottoman Empire, was certainly as powerful as the West, if not more so. However, with the second failure to capture the Austrian capital, Vienna, in 1683, they began a decline from which, most historians believe, they never fully recovered. As we shall see, this had a major impact on their scientific, technical, and cultural cutting edge. (This is the subject of Bernard Lewis's many helpful books, especially his classic *What Went Wrong?*)

A GOD DIVIDED

nineteenth century. Many of the thinkers were of Middle Eastern Christian background, including those helped by American missionaries, who founded two now-famous universities that still exist in Cairo and Beirut (in Lebanon). Many such young activists were also nationalists, wanting Arab independence from the Ottoman Empire, which was becoming more overtly Muslim and Turkish over time.[†]

In Egypt, as in the British-ruled Indian Raj, many a young Muslim nationalist wanted two things: independence from European rule and a genuinely Islamic state. What these youthful intellectuals also wished for was a return to pure Islam—the seventh-century original version, as viewed from the perspective of the nineteenth and early twentieth centuries. The founders of Islam were known as the ancestors—the *salaf*—and the desire to return to them became known as *salafiyya*.

Many of the supporters of *salafiyya* wanted to mix pure Islam with a move toward a pure, Islam-compatible form of modernity. Then, as now, the West and modernity were seen very much as the same phenomenon. Technically, medically, intellectually, and educationally, the West was miles ahead of anything in the Muslim world. These thinkers also found democracy desirable, especially since they were denied it by their European overlords, the British. (Writers such as Albert Hourani and Akbar Ahmed have written much on

---

[†] It is interesting to note that Saddam Hussein's Ba'ath, or (Arab) "Renaissance," Party, was founded by Michel Aflaq, a Syrian from the Christian minority. As of 2005 that organization, defeated in Iraq, still runs Syria.

this period, for those wanting to find out more.) Suffice it to say here that *these salafiyya* activists believed fully in democracy, the modern world, and a return to original Islam all together—and so were therefore very different from the *salafiyya* of today, such as Bin Laden.

Egypt received nominal independence in 1922, as most of the rest of the Middle East passed from Ottoman Muslim rule to European-ruled mandates, theoretically protected by the new League of Nations, but in reality under the control of Britain and France. However, as with Iraq, which also had a king and a parliament, Egypt was supposedly independent, but in practice controlled by the British. The kings played fast and loose with the nationalist movement—the *Wafd*—and the British suppressed genuine moves to true independence, especially during World War II, when Cairo was on the front line.

This proved bad news for the moderate nationalists, who were thereby unable to deliver the goods. The king was corrupt and not of authentically Egyptian ancestry. One group, however, stood out against both the king and the British—the Muslim Brotherhood.

THE ROOTS OF ISLAMIC TERRORISM

This meant there were two groups against the king and the ruling caste that mattered—secular, socialist Arab nationalists and the Muslim Brotherhood.

In 1952, the royal regime was overthrown, and the quasi-military/nationalist Arab government that has ruled

Egypt ever since took power, with Col. Gamal Nasser, the mastermind of the coup, ruling the country until his death in 1970. The Muslim Brotherhood were initially glad that the corrupt old monarchy had gone, but they soon realized that, although Nasser was nominally a Muslim, he was actually more of an Arab nationalist and socialist than a supporter of a revived Islam.

This caused grave concern to Sayyid Qutb, an Egyptian teacher and member of the Muslim Brotherhood. Since 9/11 he has been posthumously recognized as one of the most important thinkers behind the world in which we live today. His book *Milestones* is perhaps the book above all others that inspired the wave of Islamic terror we're witnessing in the twenty-first century.[†]

Qutb was no bearded, wild-eyed fanatic. He was often seen in a Western-looking suit and tie—living proof, perhaps, that appearances can be more than deceptive. What is perhaps most important of all about Qutb and many of his followers is that it's precisely because he once lived in the West that he became such an Islamic fanatic, justifying the killing of innocent people in the name of Islam.

He went to the United States not long after World War II, when he was in his early forties. He was sent by the Egyptian Ministry of Education to study American education.

[†] In terms of understanding terrorism, I have written about Qutb elsewhere, as have very able writers such as Akbar Ahmed; John Esposito; and, from a different angle, Daniel Benjamin and Steven Simon, the authors of *The Age of Sacred Terror*.

He was in several big cities, including New York, but also lived for a while in the quiet town of Greeley, Colorado.

As we saw, some late nineteenth-century followers of *salafiyya* wanted to combine devout Islam with the adoption of many modern practices that had enabled the West to gain such a march on the Islamic world. It was the religion of the West and Western countries' propensity to conquer less advanced nations with which they disagreed. If the Islamic world caught up, they could then be powerful, independent countries, devoutly Muslim on one hand and as technically, scientifically, medically, and democratically advanced as the West on the other.

Qutb saw things much differently. He was disgusted at what he saw as the gross sexual decadence of a church barn dance in Greeley. He hated what he thought was the mindless conformity behind so many streets having similar front yards. He rejected democracy totally as being incompatible with Islam. He saw modernity as the seducer of innocent Muslim minds, its attractions enticing them away from the path of true Islam. The West was the enemy.

But it wasn't so simple …

To use the phrase of one of Qutb's modern disciples, the West is the *far* enemy. What worried Qutb (and worries many Islamic extremists today) is what they call the *near* enemy. This is not the West, but the local Islamic country from which an individual Muslim may come. For Qutb and many of the senior leaders of al-Qaeda today, this was and is Egypt.

In 1981, when Islamic extremists murdered Egyptian president Anwar Sadat, they declared they had killed the pharaoh.

To us, with our interest in ancient Egyptian civilization—one especially close to Christians because of its links with the Bible—this might seem an innocuous thing to call someone. But to Islamic extremists, it's very potent. Remember, to them, Egypt was in *jahiliyya*, or unbelief, until it was conquered by the invading Muslim armies of the seventh century. Its pagan, then Christian past was now a source of shame, not pride. To be a pharaoh was to be evil, un-Islamic.

Theoretically, like Nasser, Sadat was a Muslim. But, thanks to Qutb's teaching in *Milestones*, it was perfectly lawful for devout Muslims to kill him. What Qutb was doing was twofold. First, he was reviving half of the early *salafiyya* teaching—the theological part—while rejecting the compromise with the West and modernity that the nineteenth-century advocates also endorsed. Second, he was reviving the teaching of Ibn Taymiyya of the fourteenth century that there were two classes of Muslim leaders, real Muslims and fake, and that killing or going to war with the latter was perfectly permissible for loyal Muslims, if not their duty.

So to Qutb, Nasser wasn't so much a Muslim ruler as a false one, putting Arab nationalism and socialism above true Islamic values. Under Nasser, for example, the Coptic Christian minority was first and foremost fellow Arabs and thus as Egyptian as everyone else. (The former Egyptian UN secretary general, Boutros Boutros-Ghali, is a Copt.) The Western doctrine of socialism, not the Koran, was the guiding light of Nasser's policies. Therefore, reasoned Qutb, Nasser was an enemy who had to be removed in the name of

Islam and replaced by a genuinely Islamic regime, guided by the purity of the early days of the *caliphate*. Nasser had Qutb executed for treason in 1966.

One thing we need to understand about Islam and what is going on in the Islamic world today is that the Muslim world is very far from monolithic. A major struggle is going on *within* Islam as much as there is a conflict between part of Islam and the West.

Although Qutb was executed, his doctrine lived on. Many young Egyptians were inspired, including several of the founders of what we now know as al-Qaeda. They were the people behind the murder of Sadat fifteen years later and the brains behind 9/11 twenty years after that. To them, only a state like Afghanistan under the Taliban is a true Islamic state. Not even a country as harshly Islamic as Saudi Arabia fits the criteria; and, since they reject Shiite Muslims as not properly Muslim at all, Iran doesn't count either.

At the heart of this version of Islam lies what one could best describe as sanctified violence. Unlawful Muslim regimes must be overthrown—the near enemy destroyed. Since the local enemy (Egypt, Saudi Arabia, wherever) cannot exist without support from the wicked West, the far enemy (such as the United States, Britain, Spain) must be dealt with as well. Killing innocent people, which most Muslims reject as abhorrent, is permissible if the cause is just, even if some of the casualties are fellow Muslims.

After 9/11, many will remember President George W. Bush visiting a mosque and saying that most Muslims rejected such teaching. Leading moderate Muslims such as

A GOD DIVIDED

Akbar Ahmed said the same thing. However, some Christian leaders, including John MacArthur, who wrote a thoughtful book on the subject, felt this was too simple a view.[†]

An interesting reaction was that of the late Hugo Young, main spokesman of the Catholic left in Britain and a columnist in the United Kingdom's most liberal paper, *The Guardian*. Just after 9/11 he commented that, although it was politically incorrect to say so, Islam *was* at the heart of what was going on.

To be fair to Islam, other religions also have their violent wings—for example, the mass murders of innocent Christians and Muslims in India by extremist Hindu fanatics. The decision by nominally Orthodox Serb militia forces to slaughter more than eight thousand innocent Bosnian Muslims in Srebrenica in 1995 is similarly disturbing. But—and this is the point Young was making—these are not the norm. Nor do Hindus, however fanatical, kill people outside of India; and the war in Bosnia was a local conflict, not part of a global war of Christians killing Muslims worldwide.

Unfortunately that is not the case with the kind of Islamic *jihad*, or holy war, proclaimed today by the *salafiyya* branch of Islam. It is universal, however—as deaths from New York to London and Madrid, Bali, and Karachi all remind us.

[†] I'm excluding some of the wilder statements by others, as some of them have been retracted.

A Living Faith

✡ ✝ ☪

In the winter of 2005 millions of people were lining up to see the movie *The Lion, the Witch and the Wardrobe*, the first in the Chronicles of Narnia series of books written by Christian apologist C. S. Lewis.[†] My mother would read the Narnia stories aloud to me, and I enjoyed them enormously in a childlike way. But for her, the sheer power of the allegory, of Aslan's death on the stone table for Edmund's sins, was what was most moving. Seeing the movie version many years later, I can understand what she felt then.

[†] I still treasure a letter I received from author C. S. Lewis when I was a child. I still possess it this day.

Chapter Seven

APOLOGETICS AND "TRUE TRUTH"

The strength of its apologetic is where the Christian faith remains as powerful as ever, because it alone has the truth.

This is a very politically incorrect thing to say![†]

Nonetheless, the heart of this book's message is there's only one true faith, that of Jesus Christ crucified and risen, the unique Savior.

When the Narnia film reached the cinemas in Britain, there was an enormous row in the secular newspapers, as there surely was in many similar parts of the U.S. media. Some of the British coverage was vicious, an excuse for attacking Christianity on a scale not seen for some time.

Lewis wrote he had never intended to write an allegory, and it's probably true that the story emerged with the allegory coming as a result of Lewis's faith rather than any preplanned design. But it's hard to read that novel or the story of Eustace losing his dragon scales in a later Narnia book, *The Voyage of the Dawn Treader*, without seeing a very profound allegory of Christ's saving work in human lives.

Perhaps the more overt Lewis stories are less well-known works, such as *The Screwtape Letters*. (They're not as famous in the wider community as the Narnia series, though many Christian readers know them well.) Here one can see

---

[†] Thankfully, my publisher knew what my book would say ahead of time—what I write will not be censored as so much material is these days, especially in high school textbooks. For instance, I always have to relearn what can and cannot be said when I teach at an American university each summer, although at that level much of the "speech code" is good manners rather than anything draconian or sinister.

A GOD DIVIDED

Here one can see

Lewis at his apologetic best, showing the daily struggles, trials, and temptations Christians face and the subtlety of Satan's snares, as he seeks to grind them down.

The Christian faith is a wholly realistic faith, taking human beings as they are, rather than drowning them in the legalism of a Koran or a Talmud. We cannot save ourselves; we will never be good enough; self-redemption will be forever beyond us. That is why Christ came, to redeem hopeless sinners like us, for without God's grace our position is truly hopeless.

Proper apologists always start at the beginning, as the Bible also does. I remember my time at L'Abri, the place in Switzerland founded by the late Francis Schaeffer. He always attempted to take us back to the *very* beginning—with God himself. "In the beginning, God …" is how the Bible starts, and that is how it should be. If we fail to remember even God's existence—the tragic case with many in the West today—then we are sunk from the outset.

Schaeffer was known for his many apologetic books. But he maintained that the real work of L'Abri all began with *True Spirituality*. Schaeffer had a major experience of God's truth while up in a hayloft during a very stressful period in his life, and he came across the expression that was to be a hallmark of his time in Switzerland: "true truth."

The idea of *true* truth would seem a tautology. But God gave Schaeffer this insight more than fifty years ago now, before anything such as postmodernism was even heard of. Yet it's profoundly relevant to the confused twenty-first century in which we live, where the very notion of such a thing as truth is under attack.

My wife, in reading the sermons on Isaiah by Schaeffer's friend and contemporary, the late D. Martyn Lloyd-Jones, remarked that it was amazing that sermons preached more than sixty years ago were so refreshingly contemporary. They had not dated at all, even though the 1940s were dramatically different in so many ways from the early twenty-first century.

Well-known preacher John MacArthur was once criticized for being too biblical in his sermons and not contemporary enough. His riposte was interesting—if you are biblical, you are always contemporary.

But this isn't surprising, since the message of the Christian faith has stayed exactly the same, not just for sixty years, but for nearly two thousand years, since it was first preached in first-century Palestine.

This is where Christianity contrasts so vividly with the other major universal faith, Islam, which becomes dated by its very nature.

Islam's Struggle with the Modern World

Islam is a faith in crisis. Many books have been written on this subject, especially since 9/11. However, they look at Islam not just from a secular viewpoint, but also from a political or sociological perspective.

Islam, as we saw earlier, is a religion of power. To be effective, it needs at least a sympathetic, if not an Islamic, regime. This is what Islam was designed to be from the very

A God Divided

beginning, since Muhammad first took power in Medina, where his teachings were accepted, and then, after several military campaigns, in Mecca—these two cities being the sacred heartland of Islam to this very day.

Christianity, we saw, has only rarely been geographically rooted or dependent. It's not about place, an earthly realm, but about redemption, a restored relationship with God through Christ's finished work on the cross. It's therefore independent of outward circumstances in a way that Islam is not.

Here it's important to say that many contemporary Muslims, especially those influenced by Islam's Sufi mystic side, have no propensity for violence; their brand of Islam would forbid it. But when we looked at the origins of this kind of Muslim faith, we saw that the people who introduced it no longer accepted the rather arid legalism of formal Islam.

Some, including French commentator Gilles Kepel, believe the aggressive, al-Qaeda–linked style of *salafist* violence is the last throe of a dying branch of Islam and see this kind of extremism as soon to be extinct. He and similar experts believe what we need to do is to revive the spirit of toleration seen in al-Andalus, where for a brief period the Umayyad rulers granted religious freedom to all and allowed thought, medicine, and the sciences to flourish.

Not all secular commentators agree with this sunny approach. Those with a gloomier view include Malise Ruthven, a British writer on Islam and North American religion.

Not every Christian writer would agree that there really are genuinely moderate Muslims. But there are some brave people who are doing all they can to bring about reconciliation and peace. However, fellow Christians who have disagreed with me in the past tend to be those doing a wonderful task of defending Christians who are actively persecuted in majority-Muslim regimes such as Pakistan. While moderate Muslims can certainly and genuinely exist, it is plain why they hold the point of view they do.

However, much of the crisis, as Kepel and others remind us, is in Europe, with its enormous and growing Muslim population.

Where the Kepel approach goes wrong is that in al-Andalus, the Umayyads were (a) in charge and (b) ruling over a non-Muslim majority. These two historical circumstances made all the difference. It's easy to be enlightened when one is the ruler rather than the subject. Furthermore, for the Umayyads, the Koranic dictum that there's no compulsion in religion made sense. In Iraq, for example, or Tunisia, the majority of the population converted to Islam, but not in Moorish Spain. The majority remained firmly Christian or Jewish.

Kepel wants there to be a new spirit of al-Andalus among the Muslims of modern Europe, a live-and-let-live approach that enables them to continue being Muslims while tolerating the predominantly secular character of the world around them.

This would be good if it could happen. We've seen already the pro-peace road show that Muslim sage Akbar Ahmed has in the United States with Judea Pearl, the father of murdered Jewish *Wall Street Journal* reporter Daniel Pearl.

There seem to be several categories of Western Muslims. There are first those who assimilate and adapt their Islam to the society in which they live. These are the Islamic equivalent of theological liberals, who accommodate a lot of their faith to whatever the predominant secular mind-set of the age might be. The gay Muslim Canadian journalist who wrote *The Trouble with Islam* would be in this category. Such people have a great reputation in the secular media—not surprising since they hold to secular values—but have little or no credibility with their own religious community, since they have jettisoned many of the core beliefs.

Then there are those who remain loyal to their beliefs and at the same time want sincerely to live in peace and tranquility with the West. This category has a hard time from both sides—they're too Muslim for the secularists and too nice to Westerners for many in the Muslim community.

Next are hard-line Muslims, often very outspoken in the vehemence of their beliefs, but who, nonetheless, personally reject the path of violence, even though they might (mostly in private) say they "understand" where the extremists come from. Such people want, for example, for Muslims in the West to live under Islamic *sharia* law even though they are geographically in non-Islamic nations. Frequently, such leaders denounce Western decadence, foreign policy, and much else and want everyone to convert to Islam. They can get away with saying all these things in the West because of its belief in freedom of speech. The irony is that if the same group of people tried to make the same pronouncements in many Middle Eastern countries, they would be locked up immediately, because freedom of speech is unknown there.

It's the presence of many such groups in Britain that has caused the French security services, which often take a more draconian view, to call London "Londonistan."

Finally, there are the real extremists, who have killed in the name of Allah in New York, Washington DC, Pennsylvania, Bali, Madrid, and London. The atrocities in London on July 7, 2005, acted as a considerable wake-up call. Many suddenly realized that there's a considerable community of British-born Muslims who want to kill people, not just "out there," but at home as well.

New York Times columnist Thomas L. Friedman has given the last two categories names that are helpful: the *Arab street* and the *Arab basement*, respectively. Since the Bali and London bombers were Muslims but not Arabs, one could perhaps substitute *Islamic* for *Arab*.

In his many books, University of California sociologist Mark Juergensmeyer argues that terrorism is a reaction against the forces of modernity. He also correctly spurns that much misused and abused word *fundamentalist*. He prefers to use the term *antimodernist*. Certainly, in an Islamic context, many would agree with him. (Akbar Ahmed, for example, agrees that the term *fundamentalist* is highly misleading because, since most Muslims believe the Koran to be true, they are, in that strict sense, fundamentalist. However, most Muslims reject violence, so calling Muslim terrorism "Islamic fundamentalism" is distorting the truth.)

In his books Juergensmeyer talks about religions other than Islam. He describes the kind of extremism that led a

A GOD DIVIDED

Jew to kill Israeli prime minister Yitzhak Rabin. He discusses Hindu violence against innocent Muslims and Christians in India. He also looks at the kind of dangerously warped thinking that led Timothy McVeigh to murder so many victims in Oklahoma City.

Juergensmeyer feels that all these views, mainstream or simply weird, are rejecting the modern age. They are reacting against it in an extremely violent way, killing the innocent to show the depth of their beliefs against everything the modern age stands for.

It's important to note that Muslims aren't the only ones killing the innocent. While there's a crisis within Islam, plenty of other groups also have violent fringes. Al-Qaeda and their kind are but the Muslim manifestation of a global malaise that manifests in different forms in diverse countries.

This has also been brought to our attention by Benjamin Barber, who writes about what he describes as "*Jihad* vs. McWorld." *Jihad*, to Barber, isn't just Islamic, but anything violent in the reaction to the global reach of modernity. Even the French farmers who dumped manure in their local McDonald's are, Barber thinks, part of the trend of active resistance to modernity's advance.

Christians should take heed of this. The Devil tries to fool different parts of our world in divergent ways—rampant secularist materialism in the West, Islamic extremism in the Middle East, Hindu religious violence in India. All are attempts to divert people from the one true message of Jesus Christ.

Nonetheless, as we're considering Islam here, we should concentrate on its increasing inability to cope with the rampant and expanding threat of modernity, the dominant god of our age.

WHY CHRISTIANS NEEDN'T FEAR MODERNITY

Since Islam is a religion of power, it's necessarily threatened by the advance of modernity. Christianity, which has never needed secular power, is not. Modernity is just one of the many changing threats to Christianity and, like all others, will fail. Look at how Communism failed to extinguish Christianity. In China, the gospel is stronger today than when the Communists took power nearly sixty years ago. In central and eastern Europe all attempts to wipe it out—the Soviet Union even had museums for atheism—were completely unsuccessful. In fact, it was often the continuing faith of individual Christians under terrible persecution that led many people in such parts of the world to become Christians themselves, often with dire consequences for their own freedom or prosperity.

Materialism is often more subtle in its temptations than something overtly anti-Christian such as Communism. It's sadly true that millions of people, in lands now free of Communist rule, are being swept up into secular materialism, with the desire to accumulate ever more and more, blinding them to their real need for salvation in Jesus Christ.

In the West, we have been tempted this way for decades. Because we don't see our lifestyles as an ideology—what one

A GOD DIVIDED

might call the "greed is good" mentality—Christianity continues to be threatened.

Christians can have a theology of common grace. So much of what we enjoy today is a legitimate part of this. Changes in medicine, for example, have made our lives immeasurably better than those lived just a few generations ago. Diseases that were once fatal are now cured by a visit to the doctor and a few pills. Life expectancy is much higher than it was for our ancestors. Nearly all mothers, certainly in the West, survive pregnancy and childbirth. All this is good.

So, too, are things such as the speed and economy of transportation. Once, when a family emigrated, they never saw the relatives they left behind again. Now we have airplanes, mobile phones, and the Internet. Writing books is much easier. Instead of having to print off a hard copy of the manuscript here in Britain, then sending it expensively to the United States, with shipping taking several weeks, I can save the document on my computer and e-mail it to my editor in Colorado in seconds.

All this is good news!

But of course, we live in a fallen world, and there's a strong downside to everything. Modern medicine saves the lives of thousands of mothers who would otherwise have died in childbirth, but it also enables thousands more children to be aborted every year. Mass electronic communication is for more than just keeping families in touch or enabling authors to e-mail Christian books across the Atlantic. People can download pornography or send computer viruses. Extremist groups across the world use the

Internet to keep in touch and launch terrorist operations globally.

Such things can be used for both good and evil at the same time. Much of modern technology is thus morally neutral, tools that can be used for good or ill, depending not upon the instrument itself but upon the morals of the human using it.

Remember the Reformation? The printing presses that were able to spread the good news so rapidly for the first time were swiftly used by the forces of the Counter-Reformation to try to suppress the growing Protestant movement.

Television, for example, can greatly help our prayer lives as we see what is happening in previously inaccessible parts of the world. But apart from much offensive material that is now available on television, newscasts from the Middle East have awakened a sense of Islamic solidarity in the Muslim *umma* worldwide. An Islamic audience in Jakarta in the nineteenth century would have had no idea what it was like for Muslims in, say, Egypt. Now an Indonesian Muslim can switch on the news and become radicalized instantly by seeing clashes in Palestine. Such tools have proved highly reliable for extremist Islamic recruiters everywhere.

Modernity, in other words, can work both ways. Perhaps we can distinguish between its tools—modern medicine, satellite technology—and its values. Such tools can be forces for good if used wisely, but they can also be used as weapons to harm others.

Christians shouldn't be surprised. We believe humanity was made in God's image. We also believe in original sin. We can do great things; we can commit terrible sins.

Therefore, we can separate the tools from the values. We can hail advances in modern medicine yet never forget how such progress can be warped and misused.

The dominance of secular materialism, so much part and parcel of the value system of modernity, also needn't defeat us. We know that we live in a fallen world, where the natural temptation of humanity is to sin, to rebel against God. For most of history, Christians have been a minority in much of the world. The present situation is no different; and if we, as Christians in the West, are beginning to feel a little beleaguered, that is nothing compared to the fate of countless generations of Christians before us. Read how much of the New Testament is about coping with the *inevitability* of persecution. The early church expected to be persecuted; in today's West, we have forgotten what that is like.

To be oppressed or simply scorned isn't new for Christians. However, we have to be careful that we don't, like the Laodiceans, become lukewarm in our faith. This is the great temptation for Western Christians, living as we do in an advanced, materialist, increasingly secular, consumer society. While my temptation might be expensive bookshelves rather than a second family SUV, the Devil is subtle and seeks to find our individual points of vulnerability.

In the Islamic world, Satan, even more than the United States, is the real great tempter. Subtle temptation is what scares so many Islamic leaders today about the threat that modernity poses to the Muslim world.

As Christians we know we don't fight alone against temptation. We have the indwelling Holy Spirit to help us and intercede for us. We have Jesus, our Savior, who was tempted in all points as we are yet remained perfect. God knows what temptation is like, and he has given us a whole suit of armor and the sword of the Holy Spirit (his Word) with which to fight our spiritual battles.

WHERE ISLAM FALLS SHORT

None of this wonderful assurance of divine aid and understanding exists for Muslims, nor do they have any sense of having a relationship with a God who can be truly known. Therefore, the fight for a holy life—the *greater jihad*—is a very lonely business.

Two personal reactions become possible. One is to retreat into Sufi mysticism, as Muslims of peaceful disposition do worldwide. The other is to react in anger, to lash out at the tempter, to try to destroy the source, so it does not tempt again.

Much of the psychosexual analysis carried out these days is arguably doubtful at best, especially if it seeks to explain away acts we Christians know to be sin. But some writers, such as British commentator Malise Ruthven, have some insight when they look at the lives of some recent Islamic extremists.

Such writers point out the extreme degree of separation between men and women in Islamic societies. People of the opposite sex simply do not meet each other. While the apostle Peter reminded women to dress modestly, Christians have never required women to cover up to the degree of many Islamic societies. While (as Muslim anthropologist

Akbar Ahmed points out) the full *burka* or *chador* is a local custom rather than a direct Islamic requirement, the level of segregation between men and women goes well beyond anything in any non-Islamic country.

Young men from Islamic societies are therefore deeply shocked at the way the genders mix in the West, even if it's quite harmless. For example, Sayyid Qutb was deeply outraged by an innocent church barn dance in Greeley, Colorado, shortly after World War II. Western women going to Islamic countries are warned that natural friendliness on their part can be drastically misinterpreted by Muslim men, as was the case with nurses Qutb met in the United States.

Ruthven has speculated the same might apply to young, hitherto completely segregated men from the Islamic world going to Western countries. It was interesting how many of the 9/11 bombers had lived in the West, particularly in Hamburg, Germany, a city internationally notorious for its red-light district. Ruthven and others speculate that men from segregated societies would have had a double shock in such places and, in their attempts to overcome temptation and maintain an Islamic purity, might have overcompensated by becoming Islamic extremists.

Their conversion to extremist Islam was more than just that. But there's no doubt Islam can leave vulnerable people on their own because of the lack of spiritual help afforded. Many extremists are young men at impressionable ages, often youths whose marital prospects are slender because of poverty or the lack of opportunity to meet women in the normal way. (This is by no means always the case, of course; many hard-liners are happily married men.)

Many Christian churches, by contrast, have youth groups where they hope men and women will meet fellow Christians and marry suitably Christian spouses. The church has a high view of marriage, and the twenty to thirty age range in my own church has seen many marriages—many, interestingly enough, multiracial, since our church has members from across the globe.

Slowly but surely, *imams* in the United States and Britain are waking up to the fact that their congregations expect them to behave like pastors in Christian churches. No longer are they expected merely to be teachers of the law who preach the Friday sermon at the mosque. In terms of pastoral support, this is surely a good thing for their flocks— but it shows how Islam is changing outside of the normal confines of the Islamic world.

In contrast, pastoral support was built into the Christian church from the beginning. The book of Acts and the Epistles put care for the congregation high among God-given duties—not just of the leadership, but of Christians in general. This degree of mutual support and pastoral over-sight is unknown in the Koran, except perhaps in the *zakat*, the duty of every Muslim to give alms. (Here Islamic gen-erosity should be a challenge to ordinary Christians—do we all tithe as we should? It's surely a good principle to follow.)

This reverts in turn to a principle we saw earlier. Christianity is based upon a restored spiritual relationship that followers of Jesus can have because of Christ's finished work on the cross. This is also a legal issue—our sins are forgiven, not because of anything we have achieved but because of the perfect sacrifice of Christ on our behalf.

A God Divided

However, even the most pious Muslim, seeking through the *greater jihad* to lead a righteous life, cannot ever be assured of heaven. This, alas, is one way extremist Muslims manage to recruit the young and impressionable, as Jessica Stern shows in her fascinating book *Terror in the Name of God: Why Religious Militants Kill.* Martyrs are guaranteed a direct place in heaven and thus escape the anxiety of whether or not the scales will weigh in their favor when they die.

Here one ought to say two things. First, suicide attacks are not the prerogative of Islamic extremism—the Hindu Tamil Tiger separatists have used such gruesome ways of killing for decades, notably in the murder of the former Indian prime minister Rajiv Gandhi. Second, not all Muslims agree that suicide means martyrdom, since suicide as such is expressly forbidden in the Koran. Martyrs who die in battle, not seeking to kill themselves but to fight bravely, are regarded as proper martyrs by many mainstream Muslims. Suicide bombers, who deliberately seek death, are something else. But, as Stern points out at greater length, extremist groups from Hamas in Palestine to al-Qaeda on 9/11 find many ingenious ways around the old prohibition to justify their grisly suicide attacks.

It's rightly said that the "blood of the martyrs is the seed of the church" when it comes to Christian history. But how different Christian martyrdom is!

Christian martyrs have not died blowing up pizza parlors, but as people put to death for what they believe in. (Here one should add that while there are major areas of Christian-Muslim conflict, most places in the world where

Christians continue to be martyred are not Islamic. Most Christians who died for their faith in the twentieth century probably lost their lives in China, where those putting them to death were atheists who had suppressed all religions, including Christianity.)

Above all, Christian martyrs have died at others' hands rather than their own, and the martyrs themselves were the ones who died, not innocent bystanders. As we have seen, all the attacks imaginable on the Christian church have never succeeded in wiping out Christianity.

All this is why Christianity, as we move into the twenty-first century, is not in the same global crisis that faces contemporary Islam.

The Reformation rescued Christianity from stultifying and growing increasingly inward. It also compelled the church to reconsider its global mission and get going again with spreading the news of Jesus Christ worldwide. In our present century, the fruits of that mission are being harvested, with the strongest parts of the church no longer in the West, but in the Southern Hemisphere.

This is making all the difference to the spiritual battle with the other universal, evangelizing monotheism, Islam. Christianity can no longer be seen in such countries as the religion of the white man or the oppressing colonial. It's clearly what it really always was—*the* one true faith. In fact, people in two-thirds world countries can look at the increasingly secular, white West and then at their own country, where Christianity is rapidly growing, and see that people like themselves are the ones turning in huge numbers to the truth of the gospel.

A GOD DIVIDED

In one sense, we have been here before! Although Christianity came early to Europe—as we see from the book of Acts—it was a long time before it became *primarily* a European, and then North American, faith. It is now in reality reverting to its roots, and that is all to the good of spreading the gospel. Britain now has missionaries from Central America and West Africa evangelizing the postmodern, secular British, and traditional mission agencies are finding more new recruits coming from countries of the two-thirds world and fewer from Britain or the United States. In Britain, the Afro-Caribbean churches often are growing the fastest, and this poses a major problem for the liberal elite, who like to decry and despise Christianity but feel queasy at attacking people of African ancestry.

Recently, many gospel-centered U.S. Episcopal churches have decided to come under the oversight of Episcopal dioceses in Uganda, for it's in that part of the world that the Anglican Communion has remained faithful to the Thirty-nine Articles and the foundational doctrines of the Church of England. Thomas Cranmer might be outmoded in much of England today, but his faith and biblical insights are alive and well all over the global south.

The need for Western people to go out and take the gospel to different parts of the world is still there, and the call is as vital as ever. But the fact that some of the greatest defenders of Christian faith in the twenty-first century are African archbishops or Central American Pentecostal pastors shows that the church is as alive and dynamic as it ever was. It's thriving in parts of the world where the gospel has never been heard before.

This also makes it more difficult for Islam, which for several centuries was able to propagate itself as more authentic to African and Southeast Asian cultures. If the evangelizing Christian is another Nigerian or another Indonesian, for example, the authentically international nature of Christian faith will be obvious to those hearing the message. This is tremendously encouraging, especially since the churches in the global south have little truck with theological liberalism and are sticking strongly to the true gospel message.

In fact, as Christianity enters the twenty-first century it has cause for gratitude to God and even optimism. If one compares the Christian parts of the world to the places where Christianity existed a hundred years ago, the picture is *much* more encouraging. The "true truth" of the one true faith is becoming more widely known than ever before. If the statisticians are right that half the people who have ever lived are alive now, that is truly exciting news.

Chapter Eight

WHY ISLAM IS NOT THE ONLY WORRY

✡   ✝   ☪

Post 9/11, or post 7/7 for British readers, it would be very easy to single out Islam for special attack. This would, however, be a major mistake.

While singling out Islam might be a human reaction, it's not the right response for a Christian audience, for several reasons.

EVANGELISM, NOT ANTAGONISM

After 9/11, a right-wing columnist suggested we should simply invade the Middle East and convert the Muslims to Christianity by force. Some U.S. newspapers suggested we nuke Afghanistan back into the Stone Age. This was in itself a rather misleading reaction, since the Taliban had done a very effective job of taking that poor country back into Stone Age conditions without any Western help at all.

As Christians, we know that forced conversions are entirely meaningless, since outward conformity bears no relationship to inward change. No one can be forcibly converted, since actual conversion is something an individual *wants* to do—to be reconciled to God through Christ on the cross. Mere outward change is therefore pointless, since if the person inside is not spiritually born again, there's no real difference from what went before.

We therefore want to convert Muslims to genuine Christian faith and repentance. When I said this in another book, an online Amazon reviewer referred to my views as "chilling fundamentalism." That reviewer should have gone to Taliban Afghanistan where I had a brave female cousin (with a surname different from mine) working undercover as a missionary with Afghan women. Life under the Taliban really was chilling fundamentalism, if one wishes to use that much-abused and highly misleading word.

In the West, we strongly disapprove of Islamic polygamy—a practice that is becoming less prevalent in many Muslim countries. However, some writers have asked what the difference is between Islamic polygamy and the increasing divorce rate in the West. As someone once joked, we also have polygamy—except that instead of having several wives at the same time, we simply have the same number of wives, one after the other. In other words, it's a question of the parable of the speck and the plank. Christians should remember there's much wrong in both the West and the

Islamic world—especially when talking to strict Jews or Muslims, who both have the same basic view of the sanctity of marriage that we do.

No, we want Muslims to be truly liberated with the good news of salvation in Jesus Christ, who really is the final revelation of the one true God. This means that singling out Islam for special attack is not a good idea, because it confirms in the minds of every Muslim all the bad things they're told about us by those on their own side who want the antagonism to continue.

Likewise, too, we want Jews to become Christians, especially since we have the good news that the Jewish Messiah really did come two thousand years ago, and his name is Jesus Christ. Here, too, there's enormous antagonism against evangelizing Jews, with some Jewish leaders saying that doing so is bringing back the Holocaust and trying to make Judaism extinct. On one hand, it's ludicrous that people can, for example, be a Jew and an atheist, but cease to be Jewish if they become a Christian. On the other, it's Jewish people ceasing to believe in any religion at all that is doing the most damage to the Jewish faith today. The organization called Jews for Jesus is doing a great job in spreading the word of the Messiah to today's Jews, and Christians ought to support such evangelism as much as possible, since, of course, Jesus himself was Jewish!

When it comes to the increasing numbers of Muslims living in our midst, surely it's Christian love and kindness that will win them over, rather than Islam-phobia. That is a phenomenon that will force them ever further into their own shell and make them, while living in the West, as impervious to the gospel as their fellow Muslims living in closed Islamic lands.

Christians can and should believe in what centuries of godly theologians have called "common grace." In terms of salvation, Islam is a false path. But on many issues, especially those facing us in the West, they're on the same side we are, especially in relation to the growing materialism, secularism, postmodernism, and often sheer decadence of the postreligious society we live in.

So, while in other chapters we have been accentuating the negative (to paraphrase Bing Crosby), here let us accentuate the positive.

Agreeing in Principle

On many moral issues, Muslims and Christians actually agree with each other including opposition to abortion and same-sex marriage. Muslims, to employ a now well-worn political phrase, believe passionately in "family values." So do we.

This is where Schaeffer's co-belligerence idea is so helpful. He believed Christians can be united on key moral issues with people with whom we disagree on other issues. The particular cause he had in mind was abortion, but plenty of other things worry both Muslims and Christians alike, things such as certain school issues, for example. Nonbelievers of many kinds feel good, old-fashioned morals are still relevant to the children today.

This can therefore be an entrée to talking with local Muslims and, in due time, to sharing the gospel with them as

A GOD DIVIDED

well. If they see us as friends, they're more likely to listen to us than if we denounce all of them as evil and attack Muhammad's sex life. There is, as this book has made clear, plenty wrong with Islam, but we first need to gain their hearing; otherwise, evangelism of any kind will be impossible.

For example, while there's not much danger of America becoming a Muslim country, Christians know that the strong pull of a materialist, self-centered culture can tempt us.

Here's an irony—when it comes to secular materialism, Muslims of all stripes are as against it as we are! Also, because of Islam's legalistic nature, Muslims' faith is nowhere near as strong against such temptations as the truly life-transforming, liberating power of new life in Jesus Christ can be. To me, the fact that Christians share a common foe with Islam is a wonderful opening for sharing the gospel with our Muslim neighbors, especially those living in spiritual confusion in the West.

This can be encouraging and worrisome at the same time. It is worrying, because we can be lulled into thinking, as the secular world does, that we are really all the same and that there are many paths to God. That's the classic pluralistic, postmodern approach, and ironically both devout Christians and Muslims are united in rejecting it! There's only one way to God, and the Islamic way and the Christian path are incompatible with one another, since each says it's the one true way.

It is clear why some Christians are nervous about joining with Muslims on moral issues, even if we agree with one another. We don't want to give a false impression of *spiritual* unity where none exists—one that the secular world might presume is there by seeing us standing together on certain issues.

A Tool to Open Dialogue

On the other hand, unity on what we do agree upon can be a good way of opening the doors to presenting the gospel, where Islam and Christianity very much do *not* agree. We want Muslims to be able to listen to us and not slam the door in our faces before we even get the chance to speak.

So when it comes to salvation, the glass is half empty—to pursue this analogy, only the full and living water Christ offered the woman at the well is enough. But when it comes to disagreement with secularist humanism, one could say the glass is half full: Muslims may not be Christians, but at least devout Muslims believe that there is a God who exists and that Jesus Christ was a real person who had something important to say. While we differ totally on who Jesus was and why he came, we do at least have a common religious language with which to begin a conversation. This is very different from talking to people who reject the very possibility, let alone existence, of God or who have such mushy, postmodern views that they reject the whole concept of truth. Muslims are wrong on salvation, but at least they believe that there is a truth out there to believe.

This should encourage us to believe that evangelizing Muslims should, if anything, be easier than sharing the gospel with white postmodern Westerners for whom truth and the existence of God have long since lost all meaning. It's troubling that, because of 9/11, we concentrate so much on Islam as an enemy of the gospel and forget equally dangerous spiritual enemies nearer to home. Islam is not true, but the post-Christian materialism that pervades Western life isn't either. But because it doesn't strike us as obviously alien—as is the case with extremist Islam—Christians recognize the enemy without but become ensnared by the enemy within.

For instance, it is true that some interpretations of Islam are draconian when it comes to the treatment of women; but as mentioned earlier, the clothing that Muslim women have to wear differs considerably from country to country. Even in Iran, women can go outside without male chaperones or relatives, and they do not have to have their faces covered, as women are forced to do in Saudi Arabia. In a few Islamic countries women do not even have to wear head scarves; and in Britain, those women who do will often do so because they want to identify publicly as Muslims, rather than because they are obliged to do so by severe male relatives. So when one contrasts their modesty with the skimpy clothing often worn by Western women (in the dead of winter, no less), then we can be thankful that at least some people practice a degree of restraint. And ironically, therein we might be able to find a point of commonality and understanding.

As Christians, we need to remember that no group is beyond the reach of the good news of Jesus Christ, however much our inhibitions or the dictates of political correctness might try to persuade us otherwise. We are *not* revisiting the Holocaust if we evangelize Jews or support the work of an organization such as Jews for Jesus whose main aim is propagating the good news of Jesus as the true Messiah of Israel.

Likewise, the idea that Islam is an impenetrable barrier to Christianity is simply not true. If we believe that, we are in effect saying that not even the power of the risen Lord Jesus Christ can enter some parts of the world—and that cannot be theologically correct. Furthermore, millions of Muslims are now living in the West, not in the *dar al-Islam*; and, as we have seen, this presents an as of yet nonexistent opportunity for Christians to share the gospel. There's now a crisis in Islam because of this entirely new situation. Christians should therefore make the best of the opportunity that, one could argue, God has given us by sending so many Muslims to our doorstep. Some people might be duly fearful of this new development, but we can rather take a much more positive view and see it as a God-ordained provision to enable millions of Muslims to hear the gospel freely.

One key thing Christians have to do is separate "the West" from Christianity in the minds of Muslims and pious Orthodox Jews. Linking everything that happens in the West with the Christian faith is one of the biggest hindrances to the gospel in the Islamic world. Extremist Muslims often use the decadence of much of the West as a warning against Christianity, even though Christians would be as quick to denounce and disapprove of such behavior as any Muslim *imam*.

One reason such behavior is often banned in Islamic countries is their very strict law code. Christians might

A GOD DIVIDED

strongly oppose adultery, but we no longer believe in stoning adulterers to death, as still happens in some Muslim countries. However, this too points to the true nature of the Christian faith.

Jesus spoke to the woman at the well not to condemn her, but to convince her of her need for true spiritual salvation. With the woman taken in adultery, he didn't excuse her moral crime but told her to repent. Just as important, though, he made clear that Christianity has an even higher moral standard than just physical behavior. He said even *thinking* adulterous thoughts was against the law of God. In other words, he set the bar far higher than ordinary morality does—sin isn't just wrong deeds, but a condition of rottenness *within*, a state of rebellion against God.

Muslims agree with us that a hedonistic, materialist culture is wrong. Having said that, some Muslims who felt that most deeply, such as Sayyid Qutb, went on to become extremists and the ideological brains behind terrorist organizations such as al-Qaeda. Thankfully most Muslims still reject the path to violence yet remain very confused about how they should act, especially if they're among the growing numbers of Muslims living in the West. This very confusion is a wonderful opening for the gospel. For once such Muslims, who share so many of our values, realize we are as much against the selfish, empty materialism that surrounds us as they are, then they will realize "the West" and Christianity are *not* the same after all.

When we view the sad, fallen society around us, we Christians should realize that we cannot enforce the unenforceable. What is really needed is the power of salvation, the gospel of Jesus Christ. Simply changing the law, as well-intentioned people did in the United States during Prohibition, for example, doesn't make the key difference necessary to transform society. Only *spiritual* transformation can ever change society. People must become new creatures in Christ through conversion, not compulsion.

This is something a very legalistic, state-orientated religion such as Islam does not understand. Outward conformity without inner redemption is meaningless. A faith based upon law cannot work—it takes God's grace to bring about true and lasting change within and without.

So when we talk with Muslims about the things that horrify all of us equally, we can, as time progresses, share this grace with them and act in co-belligerence against the decadence and materialism of today's society. The Bible makes it clear that we cannot do it ourselves—all our righteousness is no use when it comes to the absolute demands of God's law. Only Jesus can save individuals, and only people turning to God for salvation can redeem towns or countries. *Sharia* law will never transform a nation, for something far more profound and radical than that is needed. Only reconciliation with God through the finished work of Christ on the cross can ever be sufficient, and that is something that Christ alone offers. Once again, Christianity is the one true faith.

✡ ✝ ☪

few weeks before writing this chapter, I was called to a private, off-the-record consultation in London. Present were a retired senior army officer, a Scandinavian diplomat, and a Muslim judge.

At that time, riots were taking part in streets all over the world in response to a series of what Muslims felt were blasphemous cartoons regarding the prophet Muhammad, which had appeared in a Danish newspaper. These riots were so serious in some countries that people actually were killed. Fortunately that didn't happen in Britain, even though the authorities were most perturbed. The conversation that took place between the judge and the diplomat as a result of these riots was fascinating.

Conclusion

A CLASH OF CIVILIZATIONS?

We noted earlier the *clash of civilizations* (Huntington's theory that cultural/religious conflicts will be the major source of strife in the post–cold war world), but this conversation showed that such a theory is far too simplistic. The Muslim judge, who was no extremist, was horrified at the slogans on placards in London that said those who opposed Islam should all be put to death. This was, the judge made plain, not at all the view of mainstream moderate Muslims living in the West.

There was a clash was there, however, even though all four of us made it evident we rejected the oversimplification of Huntington's theory.

The judge was a moderate, strongly in favor of Muslims living in harmony with the West. He was keen to quote the nonviolent *suras* from the Koran that tell Muslims to live in peace with their neighbors and not coerce them into joining Islam ("there is no compulsion in Islam"). Nevertheless, he maintained belief in the "absolute truth" of the Koran, despite the wickedness of such death-threatening slogans.

The diplomat, on the other hand, came from a secular government in a largely post-Christian Scandinavian country. To him, religion is an entirely private matter with no place in public life. Religion is for the home, not the street.

The clash I witnessed was not one of religions, but rather one between those who do and do not believe in absolute truth (albeit a truth very different from the one that I subscribe to). This is the problem we are faced with today.

A GOD DIVIDED

On many issues in Britain, Muslims and Christians have much in common. I once attended a conference, mainly consisting of lay Catholics with a few token Protestants, in which there were two very contrasting speakers. One was a Catholic eco-feminist, the other a distinguished Muslim *imam*. Nearly all the Catholics in the audience preferred the *imam*—whose theology of the family was very conservative—to their supposed fellow Catholic, the radical left-wing feminist. I could understand how they felt.

All the same, Islam is undergoing a major crisis today in a way Christianity is not. Many of the Muslims we might have the pleasure of knowing really are moderates and genuinely do want to live in harmony with us. Unfortunately, such a stance puts them at risk within their own religion. Someone such as academic and peace activist Akbar Ahmed puts his life on the line every time he appears in a show of reconciliation with Judea Pearl, a Jew.

Yet, as a British Jewish commentator wrote at the time of the Danish cartoons affair, it's hard to imagine Christian mobs rampaging through the streets with placards saying that Dan Brown (author of *The Da Vinci Code*) and all who read his book should be executed for blasphemy.

If such a scenario sounds ludicrous, it's because most Christians would never contemplate such behavior. In fact, some Christians have decided *not* to hold a peaceful demonstration against a blasphemous play (*Jerry Springer: The Opera*). Their reason wasn't because they had ceased to be appalled at something so objectionable, but because they didn't want public perception linking believing Christians with Islamic mobs.

All this comes back to this book's key issues. In particular, we need to revisit the origins of our faith—Christianity—and contrast them with the beginnings of Islam.

As we saw, Christianity spent its first three centuries a persecuted, illegal, underground faith, spread by one person witnessing to another. Islam began as a state religion, its leader both a spiritual figure and a military/political ruler. The borders of Islam spread by the sword and not by word-of-mouth, although it is now evident that many of the peoples conquered by the Islamic invaders held on to their Christian faith for several centuries.

In fact, some missiologists have argued that the Roman Empire's decision to become officially Christian in the fourth century actually hindered rather than helped the spread of the gospel. This isn't to say it was a shame that persecution ended—far from it! But the perception outside Rome's borders was that Christianity was the empire's religion in the same way that, say, Zoroastrianism was Persia's official religion. When Islam came, this view only increased; even today, most Muslims living in Islamic countries still think of the West as officially Christian and think all that happens in the West is somehow linked to the Christian faith. When they see the West's high divorce rate, they don't blame the real enemy—secular selfishness—but Christianity itself.

Ironically, because the link between Christianity and the West has been successfully uncoupled in the twentieth century by the church's massive growth in the third world, the faith has spread like never before. When non-Christians see active *Korean* Christian missionaries or *Nigerian* Christian

A GOD DIVIDED

evangelists spreading the gospel, the old link between Christianity and the West is seen to be false, to the great benefit of the gospel. Even Muslims can no longer argue that Christianity is "the white man's religion," because so many clearly nonwhite peoples do so much of the evangelism today.

THE ISLAMIC CRISIS AS AN OPPORTUNITY FOR EVANGELISM

Christianity began in unfriendly, hostile circumstances. Islam began officially when Muhammad fled from Mecca to Medina and set up a state under his rule—one that included armed combat with his enemies.

This is why, of the three great monotheistic faiths, only Christianity is not in crisis. Judaism's crisis is not so much because of politics or conflict—most Jews in the world live outside of Israel, not in it. Rather the reason is that many Jews are marrying non-Jews and having children who don't observe their nominal Jewish faith. Also, Judaism is no longer a proselytizing faith. The main emphasis now is on keeping those who do profess some kind of Jewish allegiance rather than trying to win converts from other faiths.

Islam is having a huge internal crisis, both in the *dar al-Islam* and among Muslims living in the *dar al-harb*. Within the Islamic world, it is an internal clash between moderates and those whose version of their faith is toxic, as we discovered on 9/11. For many extremist Muslims, it is *other Muslims* who are the true enemy, the "near enemy"—people they regard as apostates, who therefore are worse than rank infidels from the West.

Within the Muslim diaspora, there are courageous voices speaking for peace, good neighborliness, and harmony, such as many of the Muslims in Britain and the United States. Then there are those who, while living in the West themselves, hear the siren voices of terror and kill those they live among.

Islam, we saw, is completely a religion of works righteousness. Only martyrs can be sure of getting to heaven, which is perhaps why so many sadly misguided young Muslims today sacrifice themselves needlessly in terrorist acts against innocent people. But perhaps above all, it's a faith that depends strongly on outside circumstances, above all on the existence of a political regime acting under Islamic law. It is a *religion of power*.

As Christians we know we are fallen human beings and therefore innately incapable of ever keeping God's law. (Read the book of Romans again to remind yourself why that is theologically so important.) The story of the children of Israel shows again and again that no political unit can ever possibly stay faithful, since the Israelites fell into sin and disobedience again and again.[†]

God's law and the Old Testament in fact condemn us, showing that we can never achieve righteousness on our

---

[†] As I wrote this chapter, I was reading Daniel's wonderful prayers of repentance on behalf of the Jewish people and God's answer: the promise of the true heir of David, the Messiah, whom we know now to be Jesus.

A GOD DIVIDED

own. That's why secular writers who attribute much Jewish influence to the origins of Islam may have something to their argument, even though they do not understand the spiritual implications.

In fact, one could say that Islam is a kind of misunderstood, misinterpreted development of Judaism, with a law but with all hope of a future Messiah taken out. Its version of God cannot be known and remains forever mysterious.

(Here we should remember that Muhammad, while calling himself the final prophet or revelation of God, didn't make any messianic or divine claims for himself, so there's no Messiah figure in Islam.)

In other words, Islam is a religion of works without hope and obedience without redemption or relationship. It is the Old Testament with the entire sacrificial system ripped out—everything, in fact, that so clearly prefigures Christ's work and perfect sacrifice on the cross.

That is why our attitude as Christians toward Muslims should not be one of hostility but of profound sorrow and evangelistic concern. The best Muslims seem to be much like the rich young ruler who met with Jesus—an earnest and clearly good person, who meant well and was concerned to keep the law, but who tragically never understood his true spiritual need. Yes, some Muslims hate us and want to kill us. But they're not the ones we're likely to meet—and even the extremists are sinners as much in need of the gospel as anyone else.

Muslims, like all non-Christians, are a people without hope. However, what makes them especially tragic and in special need of our prayers and evangelism, rather than our hostility, is the fact that they realize, unlike most of those around us in the secular West, that God is the answer. They know that the most important thing of all is a religious faith—a faith in the God who spoke to Abraham, Isaac, and Jacob (who are all found in the Koran with a whole host of other familiar biblical characters).

Yet Muslims do not believe in God through the only means God prescribes: the blood and atonement of Jesus Christ at Calvary. It's as if Muslims know the question but insist upon the wrong answer, a man-made answer.

The idea of God as our Father is unknown to Islam—they know he is wrathful, but they insist on seeing sin in terms of shame and legalism rather than as humanity's rebellion against a holy God. They do not see sin *as sin* and thus don't realize the nature of the broken relationship sin causes between God and the human race. Consequently, they see no need for a Savior; and the Koran certainly provides none, even though Jesus appears in its pages as a prophetic precursor to Muhammad, not as God the Son.

Recent terrorist events have made many millions aware of Islam in a way that they have not been before. Spiritually, this should be a call for Christians to engage in evangelism—or, if we don't live near Muslims, to pray for those who do. Since so many Muslims now live among us, we can do much to reach out to them with the gospel without ever leaving home.

Until I was in my midthirties, I lived, as did most Western Europeans, under the shadow of the nuclear threat and the ever-present fear that cold war might suddenly one day become all too real. Then, in 1989, all that vanished. The cold war ended without a nuclear holocaust, and the peoples of central and eastern Europe became free.

Some Christians pointed out that the glass was still half empty—we didn't see a large revival of Christian faith among those millions now politically liberated. It is fair to concede that that is true—materialism is now as rampant in those countries as it has been for decades in the West.

But on the other hand, God spared us the judgment of nuclear annihilation. Christians in those countries are no longer persecuted and can preach the gospel freely. What seemed to be the immovable Soviet monolith is no more, and Communism in Europe vanished both peacefully and effectively almost overnight.

What is now Islam's heartland was once Christian—countries such as Egypt, Iraq, and Jordan. Even Saudi Arabia once had large Christian and Jewish minorities. Is there any *spiritual* reason why that cannot be the case again? In 1988, who could have predicted the fall of the iron curtain? So what spiritual reason do we have to believe that the monolith of Islam will prove equally impervious to the gospel? For centuries the gospel got nowhere in China; yet now, despite decades of Communist persecution, it's growing more rapidly than ever before, with tens of millions of Chinese turning to faith in Christ whatever the odds and however great the human opposition.

Judaism today is facing a severe demographic challenge. Islam has a major internal crisis, both within its borders and among the millions of its adherents living in the West, especially in Europe. Christianity, by contrast, is expanding as never before, perhaps at its greatest rate of growth since the first century, and by the same means— through conversion.

Like Islam, Christianity today is a multiethnic faith. But completely unlike Muslims, Christians are used to the concept of living in a hostile world, of being persecuted, as is happening now to Christians all over the world—from Nigeria to Pakistan, from Morocco to China.

Ours isn't a religion of dead legalism, but a living faith, with a risen Savior with whom we have a personal relationship based not on our own righteousness but on what he accomplished for us. Only Christianity offers true peace and reconciliation with God.

That is why Christianity alone is the *one true faith*, the path to salvation and to eternal life.

A GOD DIVIDED

✡ ✝ ☪

CHAPTER 1

1. What does Abraham's life teach us today about how we should live in obedience to God? Can we trust God for a future we don't know and have faith that God does know it?

2. Monotheism—belief in just one God: We take it for granted today, but how do we see faith in the true God develop as the Israelites realize (a) that they should worship only one God, not many, and (b) that no other gods even exist?

3. What does that say for us, as Christians, living in a pluralistic world in which new forms of paganism are returning?

4. Even secular writers have referred to the Ten Commandments as *ethical monotheism*. What should the true basis of ethics be in our world today, and why?

5. It is evident from much of the Old Testament that just being a Jew did not save anyone. What made for a *believing* Jew, and why is that important for us today?

6. A thought to ponder: Being simply born a Jew did not save people. Does the same principle apply (a) to those

born into a Christian family and (b) to those born into countries where most people profess some kind of Christian faith?

CHAPTER 2

1. What do the chapters on Judaism tell us about the importance to us, as Christians, of reading the Old Testament? Why is it still relevant?

2. This part of Jewish history shows how God's people can go astray—what warnings do we learn from that for our own time?

3. The Jews thought they would always be God's unique people—what do we learn of their spiritual decline, even after the return from exile, that has relevance for us today?

4. How do we learn to be a people for God under non-Christian rule from the way godly Jews coped under Greek and Roman pagan rule?

5. How do we see God preparing the way for the Christian faith in the centuries before Jesus came to earth?

6. We live in a Christian country—or do we?

CHAPTER 3

1. What did Jesus Christ come to earth to accomplish? Is it easy for us to forget the centrality of the cross, and, if so, why?

2. Christianity became a multicultural, multiethnic, global faith from the beginning. Why is that significant? How do our own churches reflect that kind of mix?

3. Christians knew their faith was for everyone—do we really have such a sense of urgent mission? How can we develop

our sense of having the *only* truth through which people can be saved?

4. With Constantine, the church gained a link with the state. Is that always helpful? Let's be controversial: Is it conversion or government policy that saves people and changes individual lives?

5. With the war on terror going on, many people are talking about a *clash of civilizations*. Do you think that clash is occurring, and what should Christians do with those of other faiths around us?

6. Why is the Bible so central to Christians? How can we improve our knowledge of what God is saying to us through it?

CHAPTER 4

1. How did Islam begin?
2. How should we think of Muslims living near us?
3. What key Jewish and Christian doctrines do Muslims misunderstand?
4. Does reading about Islam improve our prayer life, and, if so, how?

CHAPTER 5

1. How would you contrast the growth of Christianity and of Islam?
2. What do you think about the Crusades? Should Christians defend them?
3. How do you see Muslim-Christian relations in our own time?
4. Has terrorism altered the way you see the world? If it has, how and why?
5. Is there a specifically *Christian* response to terrorism?

READERS' GUIDE

CHAPTER 6

1. Some people argue that the Reformation was a tragedy—what would you say in response, and why?

2. The Reformers often disagreed among themselves—where should we draw the line in our disagreements with others? What is essential for faith, and what is a less-important doctrine?

3. What has internal reformation accomplished in Judaism and Islam? Are those changes the same as the Christian Reformation, or do they make no real difference?

4. In today's climate, how can we deal with those who say that they're moderate Muslims? Should our spiritual attitude to this issue be different from our political response? If so, why?

CHAPTER 7

1. How do the fictional works of writers such as C. S. Lewis help us to convey the Christian faith to nonbelievers?

2. What role should apologetics play in our evangelism? Do we really understand our faith to be *true truth*, as Francis Schaeffer once put it, and why is that important in today's postmodern world?

3. John MacArthur said that to be biblical is always to be contemporary—do you agree? If so, why? What place does the Bible play in your evangelism?

4. What can we learn through dialogue with moderates of other faiths? Do such conversations help or hinder evangelism? Or does it depend on what we are trying to accomplish through different methods of outreach?

5. Why is Christianity expanding globally when the secularists say it should be in retreat? What can we learn for our own country about how Christianity is growing in cultures very different from our own?

A GOD DIVIDED

6. What specifically Christian response should we make to terrorism?

CHAPTER 8

1. What sins are we aware of in our own society?
2. Should Christians always defend the West?
3. What values do many in our country have that we as Christians reject?
4. How dangerous is materialism?
5. Are there shared values Christians have with Muslims?
6. If the answer is yes, what should Christians do if we agree with Muslims on some key issues (such as opposing abortion)?

CONCLUSION

1. What are you doing to meet Muslims where you live?
2. How aware are you of the rapid global growth of the Christian faith? Are you aware of where your brothers and sisters in Christ are being persecuted? If so, what are you doing to help them?
3. What are the main lessons you've learned from this book? What can you do (a) to put them in practice yourself and (b) to be sure your church does the same?

A FAITH THAT MAKES SENSE

✡ ✝ ☪

We saw in the chapter on the growth of Islam that, while science flourished early on in the great Abbasid *caliphate*, that flowering didn't last long, as it was deemed incompatible with the kind of Islam that eventually prevailed. We also saw that science in the West was able to continue to grow precisely because so many of its leading lights were Christians.

Science and religion have often been seen as incompatible with one another. Historically, this is far from the case. Christians were at the forefront of scientific discovery in the seventeenth century, and through to the nineteenth century the clergyman-scientist remained a common figure, the best known being William Paley, the British thinker remembered for his "divine watchmaker" argument for design.

FAITH AND SCIENCE: AT ODDS?

The clash between science and faith really began in the nineteenth century with, Denis Alexander and Alister McGrath both point out, the rise of the professional, full-time scientist. (Ironically, Charles Darwin himself was one of the last gentleman amateur scientists, since he didn't hold a university post.) Alexander has written a key book for Christians to read, *Rebuilding the Matrix*, and McGrath has written many helpful books, including his recent demolition of atheist scientist Richard Dawkins (*Dawkins' God*).

In the twentieth century, major scientific discoveries have been made that strongly support the compatibility between Christianity and science. The idea that the two still clash is true, one could argue, only for the biological sciences, because it is there that the dispute over Darwin still persists. In other spheres this is far from the case, including the ones I'll concentrate on here: cosmology and astronomy.

Here I should add that my sympathies tend to lie with the intelligent design school of interpretation, although I fully understand Christians who agree with the other two paradigms in which Christians believe: young-earth creationism and theistic evolution. Distinguished Bible preacher John MacArthur has written a strong defense of the first view in his book *The Battle for the Beginning*, and many Christian theistic evolutionists are in print, including Alexander, McGrath, and others. All would claim that their own views are Scripture based.[†]

In some ways it's a shame it's biology that hits the headlines, although it's probably not surprising since it was the subject of Darwin's *The Origin of Species*, which created a storm that hasn't died down to this day.

THE DNA DISCOVERIES

However, I'll mention one biological discovery, as one leading Christian scientist here in Cambridge tells me it is highly regarded science. This is the remarkable story of mitochondrial DNA, the DNA we inherit from our mothers, they inherited from their mothers, and so on.

[†] As I write this chapter, a judge in Pennsylvania has banned the teaching of intelligent design in a school district in that state. One key witness was Michael Behe, a distinguished American scientist and author of *Darwin's Black Box*.

Geneticists at the University of California Berkeley in the 1980s found something that, from a Christian viewpoint, was fascinating: *Every person alive is descended from a woman who lived an estimated 150,000 years ago*, who came to be called *Mitochondrial Eve*. Needless to say the press got very excited by this, as did Christians.

Not surprisingly, the paleontologists were upset, as the geneticists had proved their theories to be wrong. Secular scientists were discombobulated to find references to Eve, but many Christians found it fascinating.

Further research was done by Bryan Sykes, who discovered that, genetically speaking, everyone in Europe (and therefore much of the U.S. population) is descended from just seven women who lived even more recently. His book *The Seven Daughters of Eve* is fascinating from many points of view, not least because it's based on the scientific research of a secular scientist at Oxford University.

Christopher Stringer at the British Museum of Natural History, who also agrees with the mitochondrial DNA discoveries, has put forward another theory: The whole human race alive today comes from one place, which our ancestors left about 100,000 years ago to populate the rest of the earth. He, like most of the scientists in this school, believe Neanderthals are not the ancestors of today's humanity. In fact, the Neanderthals became extinct 20,000–40,000 years ago.

It's very important to say here that secular scientists would not in any way endorse the *theological* ramifications to these remarkable discoveries. But it does go to show that biology, which is usually used against religious belief (especially Christianity), is coming up with discoveries that don't do anything of the kind. Some scientists believe other people were around at the time of Eve, although there's no surviving DNA in their descendants. They give the date of "Adam" as

90,000–60,000 BC and argue the man from whom we all descend lived 30,000 years after his mitochondrial DNA ancestor, Eve. Here science would not tally with the biblical account, and we should be aware of that.

However, if you marry yourself to the trends of today, you'll find yourself widowed when the next day comes along. This should be a warning about getting *too* excited by particular scientific discoveries. Even so, Christians can feel at least encouraged with these particular findings, even if it would be wrong to let ourselves get too carried away.

It's also true that young-earth creationists would not like the 150,000-year date for Eve, although such chronology should not worry intelligent design supporters. Even so, the fact that secular scientists now believe we all descend from just one woman should be a cause for celebration.

Anthropologists and archaeologists have found that civilization— writing, agriculture, cities, and so on—is also of recent vintage, from around 5,000–6,000 years ago. Apparently they find it a puzzle that humanity suddenly became so civilized!

THE HEAVENS DECLARE THE GLORY OF GOD

However, in astronomy and cosmology, twentieth-century discoveries have put the case for believing in God back at the top of the agenda.

It is very surprising that discoveries in cosmology and astronomy have not played a pivotal role in the case for intelligent design.[†] The omission is a shame, since recent research into the beginning of the universe surely screams God's existence from the rooftops. In

---

[†] Search, for example, Dembski's seminal work; the amazing finds in that field are scarcely mentioned. To be fair, he is writing a book based primarily upon the biological sciences. Even so, it is surprising that he does not mention the mitochondrial DNA discoveries—they are impressive.

A GOD DIVIDED

the past, eminent Christians in science made discoveries every day that proclaimed, as the psalmist did, that the heavens declare the glory of God. Recent findings in astronomy do, too.[†]

Fortunately, neither Denis Alexander nor Alister McGrath makes this omission. I'm most indebted to their splendid research in much of what follows (although it does require some mathematical knowledge to read the latter's works on the history of science fully). They show that there have been Protestant astronomers since the time of Kepler and that the idea that either Luther or Calvin opposed Copernicus is completely false and entirely unhistorical.

Christians of all persuasions—young earth, intelligent design, theistic evolutionist—all thankfully agree the universe had a definite beginning! Christians in the early church also realized this, and it differentiated them strongly from the pagan religions around them. They understood, for example, that God is separate from his creation. By the fourth century, St. Augustine of Hippo fully understood God created the universe *ex nihilo*, literally "out of nothing." When, therefore, secular scientists made a similar discovery in the late twentieth century, they were only finding a scientific fact that many Christians had known for over 1,600 years! God didn't create the universe out of preexisting matter, because he created the matter out of which the universe came.

What is fascinating is that the Genesis account begins with the creation of light, as does today's scientific account of the big bang, the description secular scientists give to God's initial act.

This is in itself astonishing, since until not so long ago, many distinguished astronomers believed in what is called the steady state theory. This presupposed that the universe had always existed and

---

[†] While I'm no astronomer either, I've been interested in this field since childhood, although the mathematics involved sadly long since defeated me. But Cambridge is full of astronomers who combine distinction in research with an active Christian commitment, eminent science writer Simon Mitton being the best known.

creation of new material happened all the time. Firm evidence against the theory came in the 1960s, when two scientists, Penzias and Wilson, working at the Bell Telephone Laboratories, accidentally discovered cosmic microwave radiation, the residue of the big bang. Big bang cosmology soon became the norm and is now the main accepted theory among most astronomers, however secular their outlook.

This change is interesting because it shows scientists can completely shift their basic beliefs in the face of evidence. Few now still defend steady state, since the evidence for the big bang grows all the time, notably with the findings of the COBE satellite a few years ago, which proved that cosmic background radiation, the proof of the initial explosion, was constant around the entire observable universe.

Scientists' willingness to adapt their theories to new evidence is by no means unusual, outside of evolutionary biology. For example, we now know the part of the earth upon which we live is on massive, permanently moving plates. This is called plate tectonics. Look, for example, at South America and Africa. It's obvious they were once linked, and this is what plate tectonics tells us. However, when the theory first came it was heavily criticized and took some while to gain scientific credence. Now, however, everyone in geology believes it. (Nor is plate tectonics in any way incompatible with a Christian account of creation, in whichever of the three varieties one might believe.)

With such major cosmological discoveries, needless to say, astronomers soon began speaking of God, or at least god, since many of those using his name would not be Christian believers in any sense. The most famous example of this is famous astronomer Stephen Hawking, whose book *A Brief History of Time* has been continuously in print since it was published nearly twenty years ago and has sold millions of copies worldwide. Although Hawking isn't Christian, the book famously ends with the quote that when we finally find an overarching theory to explain our universe, we would then discover the "mind of God." This phrase was in turn taken up by Australian scientist Paul Davies, who wrote a book entitled *The Mind of God*. It's fair to say Davies' god has more in common with a Hindu deity than the true God of the Bible, but nonetheless, Davies realized scientific evidence was pointing strongly to a designed universe.

As McGrath and Alexander demonstrate, the fact that the universe is here at all, and that we are in it, is in itself remarkable. Another well-known Cambridge figure is the former Astronomer Royal, Martin Rees, who isn't a professing Christian. Nonetheless, he wrote a major work entitled *Just Six Numbers*, which showed that our universe's survival beyond the big bang is nothing short of amazing. Had just six numbers been marginally different, the universe could not exist and we would not be here either. There would have been no stars, no galaxies, and certainly no planets upon which life could live. In short, our very existence is extraordinary—or, Christians might add, miraculous.

One might think from TV shows—whether documentaries of the late Carl Sagan or science-fiction series such as *Star Trek*—that there's a unanimous consensus that life is plentiful on other worlds, if only we could somehow contact them. The entire SETI program, which Sagan (and later the movie based on his novel) fictionalized in *Contact*, is based on the belief of some scientists, called *exobiologists*, that this life exists.

However, many secular scientists are more than skeptical about this. As eminent physicist Enrico Fermi once famously asked about aliens, "Where is everybody?" While it's a matter of faith among some people that aliens are indeed out there, others take the view that such beings don't exist—unless we meet them. While we've found planets revolving around distant stars, none as yet seem the kind where life, certainly as we know it (to use the *Star Trek* phrase) can exist.

More typical of science is the book *Rare Earth*, which shows—from a secular, scientific viewpoint—that the existence of life on our planet, let alone on millions of others, is extremely unlikely. Not only does a planet have to sit the right distance from its sun, but also the star itself has to be situated in the right part of its galaxy. If it's outside the "habitable zone" in either respect, the conditions for life will not be met, since radiation levels and other cosmic horrors prevent life from even beginning, let alone developing into the kind that can send messages through space.

One thing Copernicus and his successors were supposed to have done is demonstrate that humans are much less important than we had thought. We're just ordinary life-forms in an ordinary planet revolving around a typical star in a normal galaxy.

Recent cosmology and earth science now shows that mankind could, by contrast, be *incredibly* special, since many secular scientists believe we might be alone in the universe. As far as the visible, created universe is concerned, this is what Christians have believed all along.

John Barrow, Frank Tipler, and John Wheeler wrote a complex book entitled *The Anthropic Cosmological Principle*, which highlights this view. Writers such as Alexander and McGrath have done a grand job in explaining the theory to nonspecialists, especially the very interesting theological implications for Christians. (It's a shame that intelligent design writers in the United States have not made more of this theory, because its spiritual ramifications are fascinating.)

In essence, as the theory goes: The fact that we are here and able to observe the universe around us must mean that we live in a universe in which we are possible. Since the odds against us existing at all are so great, then the whole universe must have been fine-tuned to enable us to be here.

In other words, the paradigm science has had since Copernicus—that we humans are not terribly important—has

A GOD DIVIDED

been turned on its head. Our existence as humans is of vital relevance to the universe we inhabit. Not only that, but the universe has to be as big as it is precisely for us humans on earth to live in it. For not only do we have to be the right distance from our sun and our sun be in the right part of the galaxy, but our galaxy has to be in the right part of the universe as well.

Most of us, not being eminent Oxford and Cambridge scientists, might find all this slightly mind-blowing.[†] But while the complexity of such discoveries is beyond me, too, I do think that this is all something Christians have good cause to be profoundly excited about.

We do have to be careful to avoid a "god of the gaps" approach. This means attributing to God things we don't at present understand, but which may be explained by a nontheistic, naturalist interpretation in the future. This is never helpful, from a Christian point of view. Nonetheless, since so many secular scientific discoveries confirm a Christian view of God's universe, a small degree of rejoicing should be allowed. At the very least, it shows that a Christian outlook and mainstream science need not conflict with one another and that, if anything, scientific discoveries are moving toward us rather than away.

Obviously, secular scientists would not draw the *theological* conclusions from their discoveries that Christians do.[††] Clearly atheists will always deny the theological ramifications of their discoveries and do so because they reject Christian faith. Christians might be very excited by seeing proof of God's design in the universe; but secular people of all kinds, scientists included, will not see it until the Holy Spirit opens their eyes and leads them to conversion.

[†] Although I do have degrees from both these places, I am, as I always introduce myself in such circles, a "mere historian."

[††] William Dembski reminds us of something that the evangelical philosopher Alvin Plantinga has said: that if you believe only in materialistic naturalism, then materialistic evolution is the only show in town.

The new findings in cosmology are a case in point. Martin Rees, for example, believes in the unlikelihood of life in our universe. But, like similar scientists, he now believes in a multiverse—that what we live in is one of millions of universes, all of which are invisible from one another, and in many (if not most) of which life does not exist.[†]

Spiritually, we shouldn't be surprised by such reactions. When eighteenth-century astronomer Laplace was asked why he didn't mention God in his book, he said he had no need of that hypothesis. However, God has certainly made a major comeback in recent years. Needless to say, this is profoundly challenging to those who hold to a materialistic, naturalist, atheist worldview. Once a theory makes God more likely, antireligious scientists will always want to find a get-out-of-jail clause that somehow suddenly makes God less likely or necessary after all.[††]

In any case Alexander shows, if other universes exist—even if by definition we cannot ever find them—that doesn't get rid of the issue of what happened before any of them were created. There must have been a beginning baby universe, even if it was not ours. Furthermore, other parallel universes connected by invisible cosmic membranes cannot disprove the Christian account of creation, since we know heaven exists, even if we cannot now see it with our own eyes.

In short, recent scientific discovery is very exciting from the Christian viewpoint and demonstrates the ongoing credibility of the one true faith, historical Christianity.

[†] String theory is part of this notion of many universes; and, I must confess, when astronomers try to explain it to me over coffee in Cambridge, my mind begins to boggle....

[††] This is what string theory and talk of cosmic membranes does with the fact that the universe had a definite beginning. Even secular scientists such as the famous Richard Feynman concede that before the big bang no such thing as time existed. (In which case, as Alexander and McGrath point out, they are in full agreement with St. Augustine, 1,600 years ago.)

A GOD DIVIDED

Index

A GOD DIVIDED

Ahmed, Akbar. *Islam under Siege*. Cambridge, UK: Polity Press, 2003.

Alexander, Denis. *Rebuilding the Matrix: Science and Faith in the 21st Century*. Grand Rapids: Zondervan, 2003.

Barrow, John D., Frank J. Tipler, and John A. Wheeler. *The Anthropic Cosmological Principle*. New York: Oxford University Press, 1988.

Benjamin, Daniel, and Steven Simon. *The Age of Sacred Terror: Radical Islam's War against America*. New York: Random House, 2003.

Catherwood, Christopher. *Whose Side Is God On? Nationalism and Christianity*. New York: Church Publishing, 2003.

Douglas, J. D. *The Illustrated Bible Dictionary*. Downers Grove, IL: InterVarsity Press, 1998.

Feiler, Bruce. *Abraham: A Journey to the Heart of Three Faiths*. New York: Harper Perennial, 2004.

Huntington, Samuel P. *The Clash of Civilizations and the Remaking of World Order*. New York: Simon and Schuster, 1998.

Johnson, Paul. *A History of the Jews*. London: Weidenfeld and Nicolson, 2001.

Lewis, Bernard. *What Went Wrong? The Clash between Islam and Modernity in the Middle East*. New York: Harper Perennial, 2003.

MacArthur, John. *The Battle for the Beginning: Creation, Evolution and the Bible*. Nashville: Thomas Nelson, Inc., 2005.

Manji, Irshad. *The Trouble with Islam: A Muslim's Call for Reform in Her Faith*. New York: St. Martin's Press, 2004.

McGrath, Alister. *Dawkins' God: Genes, Memes, and the Meaning of Life*. Malden, MA: Blackwell Publishing, Inc., 2004.

Rohl, David. *A Test of Time: The Bible—from Myth to History*. London: Arrow Books, 2001.

Sanneh, Lamin. *Piety and Power: Muslims and Christians in West Africa*. Maryknoll, NY: Orbis Books, 1996.

Stern, Jessica. *Terror in the Name of God: Why Religious Militants Kill*. New York: Harper Perennial, 2004.

Sykes, Bryan. *The Seven Daughters of Eve: The Science That Reveals Our Genetic Ancestry*. New York: W. W. Norton & Company, 2002.

Tibi, Bassam. *The Challenge of Fundamentalism: Political Islam and the New World Disorder*. Berkeley, CA: University of California Press, 2002.

Bibliography